Scaling Your Node.js Apps

Progress Your Personal Projects to Production-Ready

Fernando Doglio

Apress®

Scaling Your Node.js Apps: Progress Your Personal Projects to Production-Ready

Fernando Doglio
La Paz, Canelones, Uruguay

ISBN-13 (pbk): 978-1-4842-3990-2   ISBN-13 (electronic): 978-1-4842-3991-9
https://doi.org/10.1007/978-1-4842-3991-9

Library of Congress Control Number: 2018964431

Managing Director, Apress Media LLC: Welmoed Spahr
Acquisitions Editor: Louise Corrigan
Development Editor: James Markham
Coordinating Editor: Nancy Chen

Cover designed by eStudioCalamar

Distributed to the book trade worldwide by Springer Science+Business Media New York, 233 Spring Street, 6th Floor, New York, NY 10013. Phone 1-800-SPRINGER, fax (201) 348-4505, e-mail orders-ny@springer-sbm.com, or visit www.springeronline.com. Apress Media, LLC is a California LLC and the sole member (owner) is Springer Science + Business Media Finance Inc (SSBM Finance Inc). SSBM Finance Inc is a **Delaware** corporation.

For information on translations, please e-mail rights@apress.com, or visit http://www.apress.com/rights-permissions.

Apress titles may be purchased in bulk for academic, corporate, or promotional use. eBook versions and licenses are also available for most titles. For more information, reference our Print and eBook Bulk Sales web page at http://www.apress.com/bulk-sales.

Any source code or other supplementary material referenced by the author in this book is available to readers on GitHub via the book's product page, located at www.apress.com/9781484239902. For more detailed information, please visit http://www.apress.com/source-code.

Printed on acid-free paper

To my wife, who's been an amazing rock throughout this entire process: You make me a better person.

To my kids: you managed to fill a place in my heart I didn't know I had empty. I love you.

Table of Contents

About the Author

 **Fernando Doglio** has worked as a developer for the past 13 years. In that time, he has come to love the Web, and has had the opportunity to work with most leading technologies, such as PHP, Ruby on Rails, MySQL, Node.js, Angular.js, AJAX, REST APIs, and others. For the past four years Fernando has also been working as a Technical Manager and Technical Lead for Big Data projects.

In his spare time, Fernando likes to tinker, learn new things, and write technical articles and books such as this one. He's also a big open source supporter, always trying to bring new people into it. When not programming, he can be seen spending time with his family.

Fernando can be contacted on Twitter @deleteman123 or online at www.fernandodoglio.com.

About the Technical Reviewer

Shane Hudson is a freelance web developer and author of *JavaScript Creativity* (Apress, 2014). From small proof of concept prototypes to large startups, charities and government organizations, Shane has worked on all kinds of projects and with all kinds of teams around the world. He can be found on his personal site at `https://shanehudson.net` or on Twitter at `https://twitter.com/ShaneHudson`.

Acknowledgments

I'd like to thank the amazing technical reviewer involved in the project, Shane Hudson, whose great feedback was a crucial contribution to the making of this book.

I'd also like to thank the rest of the Apress editorial team, whose guidance helped me through the process of writing this book.

Introduction

Any piece of software that either deals with an increasing amount of data or interacts with the public on a world-wide capacity will eventually (if the creators play their cards right) grow out of control.

This situation can get out of hand quickly if you're not expecting it, after all, it's plays a major role in crashing your favorite websites everyday. The key aspect here, is to understand why they happen and the kind of tools you have a your disposal to solve them once they do. By getting that part right, you'll be ready to understand the signs and know how to react to them. And that is what this book attempts to answer.

Throughout this book, with the help of plenty of diagrams and, in some weird occasion, a few code samples, I'm going to provide you with the what, the where, the when, the who, and the "uh?" about scaling large platforms, while working with Node.js.

CHAPTER 1

The Need to Scale

To talk about scaling platforms and growing your application to handle whatever requirements you can think of, we first need to understand the different factors that can trigger the need to scale. These factors don't have to act together in a perfect-storm scenario to become a real headache. With only one of them present, you're done; you need to either start scaling or say goodbye to the stability of your system.

In this chapter, I'll go over the most common scaling triggers that might pop up during your application's development lifecycle, or even after going live.

External Factors

External factors are the ones you can't control. Yes, they can be expected, and you can and should plan accordingly. You can even predict them, given the right amount of data. But you don't really have a say as to whether they happen or not.

The two most common external factors that will trigger your need to scale are a considerable change in the traffic your application receives and an increase in the data you need to process.

Let's quickly go over them individually.

Traffic Increase

This is probably one of the most obvious and common cases where in getting what you wanted, you end up regretting ever asking for it.

© Fernando Doglio 2018
F. Doglio, *Scaling Your Node.js Apps*, https://doi.org/10.1007/978-1-4842-3991-9_1

Let's say you made a post in Hacker News about your brand-new app, and it suddenly got the attention of way too many people. Or maybe you published a new mobile app into Google's Play store and it was featured, and now your APIs are receiving 400% more traffic than you expected for the first five months. Or maybe your online massive multiplayer game is now popular and even though your game servers are able to handle the load, your tiny log server is crashing every 2 hours from the amount of internal traffic it's receiving.

With any of these, you now have a problem. It might directly affect your entire application, or it might be a challenge for only part of it, but you will have to fix it if you want your platform to perform as expected.

An increase in incoming traffic could affect your system in different ways; we can describe these as direct or indirect.

Direct Effects

The most obvious direct effect is overloading your servers' capacity to handle incoming traffic. No matter how good your server hardware is, if you have only one server (or a limited number of them), you'll be limited by it. Even if you were running a web application and had a very well-configured Apache server, so that you made the most of your resources, your capacity to handle traffic would still be limited by the number of processors and amount of RAM you paid for. There is no other way around it.

Particularly, Apache Httpd spawns a new process for every request, so multiple concurrent requests might cause this scenario to get out of hand quickly. Nginx, on the contrary, has a non-blocking I/O approach (much like Node.js), so it is capable of managing high levels of traffic with constant memory consumption. With this in mind, swapping them out might seem a good idea, but eliminating the bottleneck on your web server might prove to expose one in your own application.

In the following chapters I'll go over different techniques to overcome this, but rest assured, they will at some point imply spending more money on more hardware.

Indirect Effects

An increase in traffic can affect your application indirectly by overloading one of your internal processes. In a microservices-based architecture, the communication between services needs to be carefully planned. The fact that you're capable of handling the increased traffic on your user-facing service doesn't mean the rest of your architecture will be able to handle it.

Figure 1-1 shows exactly that case, where a resource-bound log server is crashing randomly and limiting the number of logs properly saved in your database. Good luck troubleshooting any other issues or bugs in your platform when that happens.

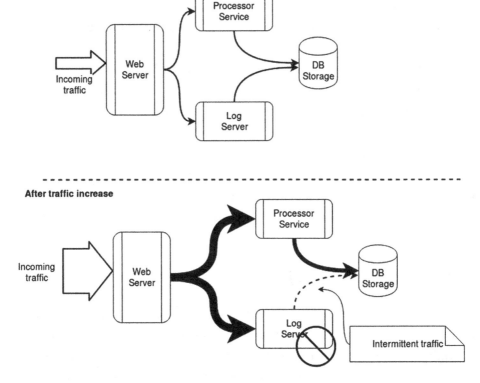

Figure 1-1. *Before and after a traffic increase affecting your platform indirectly through the log server*

3

Another possible indirect effect occurs when an increase in traffic starts affecting the performance of a service you share with other platforms. This is what is normally known as *service degradation*, when the service is still active and working, but is responding slower than usual.

In this scenario, your lack of planning and scaling capabilities will start affecting those who use your service. This is why you always want to make sure that whenever you depend on third-party services, they can actually assure you that their service will not be degraded by anything.

Increased Processing Power Required

A need for increased processing power could be related to the previous case, and sometimes can even be caused by it; but it can also develop independently, which is why it's worth discussing as a whole different category.

Specifically, this is purely a resource-related problem; you're trying to process more information than your current resource utilization technique allows you to ("trying to bite off more than you can chew"). Notice that I didn't blame the server directly; instead, I'm sharing the blame between you and your server.

In this scenario, you're trying to do *something* with one or more sources of data, and suddenly, they start providing considerably more data than you expected. And when this happens, things can go wrong in one of two ways: your service may be degraded, or it may crash completely.

Your Service Is Degraded

In the best-case scenario, even though you weren't completely prepared for the increase, your architecture and code are capable of coping with it. You're obviously being negatively affected by it, but your service is still running, although slower than usual. Once again, you've got a mob of angry users. That's right; they're coming, especially anyone who is paying for your services and suddenly not getting what they're paying you for.

In an ideal world, you don't want this scenario to happen, of course; you want your platform to be able to handle any kind of increase in the size of your data sources, and I'll cover that in future chapters. But trust me—compared to the alternative, you've got it easy.

Your Service Is Dead

If you were so naive as to think a complete failure would never happen (it happens to the best of us), then most likely your system will end up in this category. Your service is crashing every time it tries to process the new data; and what's even worse, if the source of the data has some kind of retry mechanism, or you automatically start reprocessing the data after a restart, your system is going to keep crashing, no matter how many times you auto-restart it.

Once your data-processing service starts failing like this, it could affect the rest of your platform in many ways:

- Is your platform a black monolith of code? Then your whole platform is doomed (of course, it was already doomed if you went with a monolithic approach).

- Is your service or its output used directly by your clients? You're definitely in trouble here. If you're designing an app/service/platform/whatever that people need to pay to use, you definitely need to think about scaling techniques for your first production version, no matter what.

- Is your service used internally by your own platform? Maybe you're in luck here, especially if your platform is capable of recovering from a failed service.

- Is your service logging during this endless rebooting and crashing loop? If it is, you might compromise your logging system through an increase in traffic from a crashing faulty service. Then an increase in processing needs causes an increase in internal traffic and you have two problems, maybe more if you have a non-scalable centralized logging system. Now you've compromised every component of your platform that needs to save a log (which ideally would be all of them). See where this is going?

These are some of the most common external factors that might trigger the need to scale on your platform. But what about your own requirements for the platform? Let's call them *internal factors*.

Internal Factors

Internal factors are closely related to the external ones just discussed. But instead of having them laid down on top of us, we're the ones pursuing them. That's because they provide positive benefits to the application, even though they require extra work (and sometimes not only from a scaling perspective). And they are traits you should always aim for in your architectures, unless the applications don't provide a very sensitive service to anyone.

Of course, I'm talking about fault tolerance (FT and high availability (HA). At first glance, these two terms might seem to describe the same thing, but they're slightly different concepts. Let's go a bit deeper into each one.

High Availability

For an architecture to be highly available, it must ensure that whatever service it provides will always be available and will not lose performance, despite having internal problems (such as a loss of processing nodes). The availability of a system is usually also known as its *uptime*, and commercially for service providers you sign onto an SLA (Service Level Agreement) which is measured in "nines" of availability. For instance, Amazon ensures three nines of availability for their S3 service, which in practice means they ensure 99.9% of monthly availability. Put another way, if their service fails more than 43.2 minutes a month, then they'll be over service credits. More critical services, like mobile carriers, ensure five nines of availability, which translates to 99.999% of uptime, which in turn, translates to 5.2 minutes a year of downtime allowed.

There are several techniques that can be used to achieve this, but the most common one is the master-slave pattern.

You will often see this pattern discussed while reading about database scaling configurations, since most of them tend to go this route. It basically consists of having at least one more node for each of your main ones, and some kind of monitoring on the main nodes, so that if they go down, you can promote one of these "extra" nodes into a main one. In Figure 1-2, you have a standard three-node service, where node 3's input depends on node 2's output, and node 2's input depends on node 1's output. You can also see the "slaves," which are the smaller dotted boxes next to them.

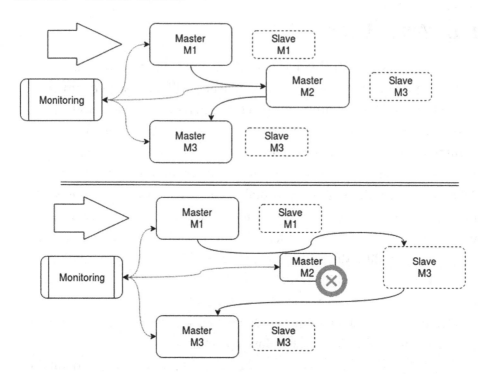

Figure 1-2. *The failure on "Master M2" does not affect the entire system*

The final component of the master-slave model is the monitoring service, which makes sure all master nodes work correctly.

The second half of Figure 1-2 shows what happens when one of the nodes fails (in this case M2). Its slave node is promoted to master (essentially taking the place of M2, connecting M1's output into its input and its output into M3's input).

In practice you normally don't need to worry about switching the connections or manually monitoring nodes for that matter; usually load balancers are used between nodes to do exactly that, act as "fixed" points of connectivity and decide by themselves (and a set of conditions you configure on them) whether or not to promote a slave.

That works well if your nodes are simple processing nodes; in other words, if you can simply exchange a master for a slave without any loss of data or any kind of information on your platform. But what happens if your nodes are part of a storage system, like a database? This scenario is slightly different from the previous one, because here, you're not trying to avoid a lack of processing power, or a processing step in your flow. You're trying to prevent data loss, without affecting your performance at the same time.

In this case, what you'll want between your master and slaves (you could potentially have more than one slave per master), is a passive data-replication process (write only) from your master into your slaves. This will make sure that if your master is lost at any point, your slaves will be able to take over with minimal negative effects, as shown in Figure 1-3. (Note that you can't prevent the master going down in mid-write, which would negate the transaction, preventing the data transfer from completing.)

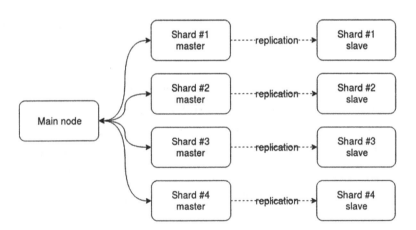

Figure 1-3. *Data replication between master and slaves to avoid data loss*

In some cases, like Redis (with Sentinel enabled), slaves are not just there waiting to be promoted, they're used for read-only queries, thus helping shed some load off their masters, which in turn, take care of all the write operations.

MongoDB, for another example, provides something called *replica sets*,[1] which allow you to set up a group of nodes, in which one of them is the primary and therefore the one your code is constantly talking to, but if something happens to it, the secondary nodes will "elect" one of them to be the new primary (as seen in Figure 1-4).

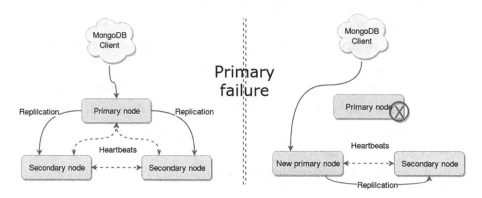

Figure 1-4. *Topology change on a replica set once the primary node fails*

Finally, another real-world example of HA is the newer versions of Hadoop's HDFS. Prior to version 2, the HDFS (or Hadoop Distributed File System) had a single point of failure in its only NameNode. In other words, if that machine were to fail or be brought down due to maintenance, the entire cluster would be rendered inaccessible until it was brought back up. In newer versions, there is an option to set up as many redundant secondary NameNodes as you want. With this feature, these nodes effectively act as passive slaves to their master, getting sufficient state (via external services called *journal nodes*) to provide a fast failover if required (shown in Figure 1-5).

---

[1]See https://docs.mongodb.com/manual/core/replica-set-high-availability/

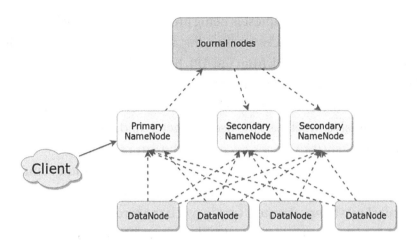

Figure 1-5. *HDFS high availability setup*

As a side-note, all DataNodes need to send heartbeats to all NameNodes to ensure that if a failover is required, it will happen as fast as possible.

As you can see, the slave-master approach can have slightly different implementations, but if you dig deep enough, they all end-up being the same.

Let's take a look now at fault tolerance, to understand how it differs from HA.

Fault Tolerance

You can think of fault tolerance as a less strict version of HA. The latter was all about keeping the offline time of your platform to a minimum and always trying to keep performance unaffected. With FT, we will again try to minimize downtime, but performance will not be a concern—in fact, you could say that degraded performance is to be expected.

That being said, the most important difference between these two is that if an error occurs during an action, a highly available system does not ensure the correct end state of that action, while a fault-tolerant one does.

11

For example, if a web request is being processed by your highly available platform, and one of the nodes crashes, the user making that request will probably get a 500 error back from the API, but the system will still be responsive for following requests. In the case of a fault-tolerant platform, the failure will somehow (more on this in a minute) be worked-around and the request will finish correctly, so the user can get a valid response. The second case will most likely take longer, because of the extra steps.

This distinction is crucial because it will be the key to understanding which approach you'll want to implement for your particular use case.

Usually fault-tolerant systems try to catch the error at its source and find a solution before it becomes critical. An example of this is having mirrored hard drives in case one of them fails, instead of letting a single drive fail. That would require replacing the entire server, affecting whatever actions the server could have been performing at the time.

Hardware-level fault tolerance is beyond the scope of this book; here, I will cover some of the most common techniques used to ensure FT at a software level.

Redundancy

One way to design fault-tolerant architectures is by incorporating redundancy into your key components. Essentially, this means that you have one or more components performing the same task and some form of checking logic to determine when one of them is has failed and its output needs to be ignored.

This is a very common practice for mission-critical components, and it can be applied to many scenarios.

For example, in 2012, SpaceX sent its Dragon capsule to berth with the International Space Station. During the ascent, the Falcon9 rocket used suffered a failure on one of its nine Merlin engines; and thanks to the implemented redundancy, the onboard computer was able to reconfigure the other eight engines to ensure the success of the mission.

Because these systems are so complex to code and to test, the cost-benefit ratio is not always something the normal software project can handle. Instead, these types of systems are usually present in critical applications, where human lives might be at risk (such as air traffic controllers, rocket guidance systems, and nuclear power plants).

Let's go over some techniques to provide software redundancy and fault tolerance.

Triple Modular Redundancy

Also known as triple mode redundancy, TMR is a form of redundancy in which three systems perform the same process and their results are checked by a majority voting system that in turn produces a single output (see Figure 1-6). If one of the three systems fails, then the other two will correct it by providing the accurate output to the voting system.

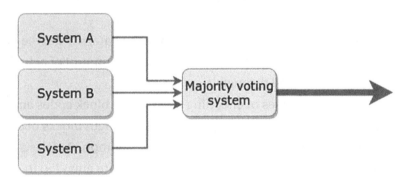

Figure 1-6. *Generic example of a triple modular redundancy system*

This is a particular implementation of the N-modular redundancy systems, where as you might've guessed, you can add as many parallel systems as you see the need for, in order to provide a higher degree of fault tolerance for a given component. A particularly interesting real-world use case for this type of solution (in this case a 5-modular redundancy system) is the FlexRay[2] system.

FlexRay is a network communication protocol used in cars; it was developed by the FlexRay Consortium to govern onboard car computing. The consortium disbanded in 2009, but the protocol became a standard. Cars such as the Audi A4 and BMW 7 series use FlexRay. This protocol uses both data redundancy, sending extra information for problem detection purposes as metadata in the same messages, and structural redundancy in the form of a redundant communication channel.

Forward Error Correction

Yet another way to add a form of redundancy to the system, Forward Error Correction (FEC) adds redundancy into the message itself. That way, the receiver can verify the actual data and correct a limited number of detected errors caused by noisy or unstable channels.

Depending on the algorithm used to encode the data, the degree of redundancy on the channel may vary and with it, the amount of actual data that can be transferred through it.

There are two main types of encoding algorithms: block codes and convolutional codes. The first kind deals with fixed-length blocks of data, and one of the most common algorithms is Reed-Solomon. A classic example of this is two-dimensional bar codes, which are encoded in such a way that the reader can withstand a certain number of missing bits from the code.

Another very interesting real-world example of this type of redundancy can be found on the messages sent by the Voyager space probe and similar probes. As you can imagine, the communication with these devices can't

---

[2]See https://en.wikipedia.org/wiki/FlexRay

really afford retransmissions due to a faulty bit, so this type of encoding is used to ensure that the receiving end takes care of solving as many errors caused by a problematic channel as it can.

By contrast, convolutional codes deal with streams of arbitrary length of data, and the most common algorithm used for this is the Viterbi algorithm. This algorithm is used for CDMA (Code Division Multiple Access) and GSM (Global System for Mobiles) cellular networks, dial-up models, and deep-space communications (sometimes it's even used in combination with Reed-Solomon to ensure that whatever defect can't be fixed using Viterbi is fixed using R-S).

Checkpointing

Checkpointing is yet another way to provide tolerance to failure; it is in fact one method that is commonly used by many programs regular users interact with daily, one of them being word processors.

This technique consists of saving the current state of the system into reliable storage and restarting the system by preloading that saved state whenever there is a problem. Rings a bell now? Word processors usually do this while you type—not on every keystroke; that would be too expensive, but at preset periods of time, the system will save your current work, in case there is some sort of crash.

Now, this sounds great for small systems, such as a word processor which is saving your current document, but what about whole distributed platforms?

Dealing with Distributed Checkpointing

For these cases the task is a bit more complex because there is usually a dependency between nodes, so when one of them fails and is restored to a previous checkpoint, the others need to ensure that their current state is consistent. This can cause a cascade effect, forcing the system to return to the only common stable state: its original checkpoint.

There are already some solutions designed to deal with this problem, so you don't have to. For example, the tool DMTCP (Distributed MultiThreading CheckPointing), provides the ability to checkpoint the status of an arbitrary number of distributed systems.

Another solution, which is used in RFID tags, is called Mementos. In this particular use case, the tags don't have a power source; they use the environment background energy to function, and this can lead to arbitrary power failures. This tool actively monitors the power levels, and when there is enough to perform a checkpoint, it stores the current tag's state into a nonvolatile memory, which can later be used to reload that information.

When to Use?

This technique is one that clearly doesn't work on every system, and you need to carefully analyze your particular needs before starting to plan for it.

Since you're not checkpointing every time there is new input on your system, you can't ensure that the action taking place during the error will be able to finish, but what you can ensure is that the system will be able to handle sudden problems and will be restored to the latest stable state. (Whether that meets your needs is a different question.)

In cases such as a server crash during an API request, the request will most likely not be able to complete; and if it's retried, it could potentially return an unexpected value because of an old state on the server side.

Byzantine Fault-Tolerance

I intentionally left this one for last, because it could be considered the sum of all of the above. What we have here is the "Byzantine Generals Problem", basically a distributed system where some components fail, but the majority of the monitoring modules can't reach a consensus. In other words, you're in trouble.

Figure 1-7 shows a basic and high-level example of what this problem means for a platform architecture. In it, you have five replicas of the component C, which send their output to four different status checkers

(A, R, M and Y), they in turn, exchange "notes" and try to reach a consensus regarding the data they all received. But because there is a problem, maybe with the data channel or with the fifth component, different values are sent to different checkers, so in this case a majority consensus can't be reached.

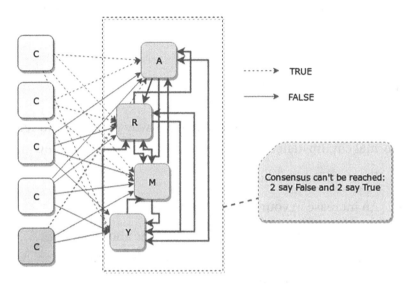

Figure 1-7. *Example of a Byzantine problem, where there is a faulty component sending random data*

There are different approaches to tackle this type of problem; in fact, there are too many out there to cover in a single chapter, so I'll just go over the most common ones, to try to give you an idea of where to start.

The simplest approach, and it is not so much a solution as a workaround, is to let your status checkers default to a specific value whenever consensus can't be reached. That way, the system is not stalled, and the current operation can continue.

Another possible solution, especially when the fault is on the data channel and not on the component generating the message itself, is to sign the messages with some sort of CRC algorithm, so that faulty messages can be detected and ignored.

Finally, yet another approach to ensure the authenticity of the message sent is to use blockchain, just as Bitcoin does, with a Proof of Work approach, in which each node that needs to send a message must authenticate it by performing a heavy computation. I'm simply mentioning this approach, since it could be the subject of an entire book, but the idea behind this approach is that it solves the Byzantine Generals problem without any inconvenience.

Summary

To sum things up, there are a couple of reasons why you'd want to scale under normal circumstances, and they're usually tied to the following:

- Your traffic increasing.

- An increase in your processing needs.

- Some form of side effect from one of the above (such as a faulty log server caused by the increased traffic your whole platform is getting).

- Or you're looking for a very specific side effect from your actions, such as high availability or fault tolerance.

The next chapter will cover some of the most common architectural patterns. We might revisit some of the ideas covered here, but we'll look at them from a different point of view.

CHAPTER 2

Architectural Patterns

Creating a scalable architecture is not just about drawing boxes on a whiteboard and then connecting them with black lines. There is usually a method to the madness, and in this chapter I'll show you some of the common patterns used in creating a professionally designed system.

In other words, I will provide you with a building block for your next big project, and even if none of the examples presented here exactly suits your needs, you'll be able to solve your problems using the tools you picked up in this chapter.

The Patterns

The IT field is filled with patterns, which is funny if you think about it, because we usually take pride in the way our work is so much like a work of art, where imagination plays such a big role. Little does everyone else know that in fact, we're just using tried and tested patterns and adding little changes to make them work for us.

Yes, it's true, every once in a while, there comes a new da Vinci and blows our mind with a completely new and original pattern. It can happen, and it will happen, but in the meantime, the rest of us can take pride in our originality while we blindly follow the work of others.

And please, don't take this the wrong way. This is exactly what we should be doing. We're not paid to reinvent the wheel every day, in fact, we're paid to solve problems in the most efficient way, and what's more efficient than re-using someone else's solution if it fits our needs? Literally nothing.

© Fernando Doglio 2018
F. Doglio, *Scaling Your Node.js Apps*, https://doi.org/10.1007/978-1-4842-3991-9_2

So without further ado, let's start getting our hands dirty with the different architectural patterns I'm going to cover in this chapter.

Layered Architecture

One of the most common patterns is probably the layered or *n*-tier architecture pattern. It is based on the logical separation of concerns of your application (or platform) into layers. And these layers must comply with the following points:

- Each layer must have a well-defined purpose (presentation layer, business layer, and so on).

- Each layer cannot speak (or send data) to any other layer that is not the one directly below it

---

Tip   In most publications, the terms *layer* and *tier* are used interchangeably, but in practice they refer to two different topics. Layers are logical groupings of your code, while tiers refer to physical instances (that is, servers) where the code resides. This is relevant, because you could perfectly well have a 3-layered architecture that is deployed into a single tier (your developer's workstation).

Figure 2-1 shows a very high-level overview of how this pattern expects the layers to be organized. The level of abstraction, as shown in the image, refers to the specifics of the business that the logic for your application is built around. In other words, the deeper you go into your layers, the more detail you'll have to deal with regarding your specific business data model and business rules.

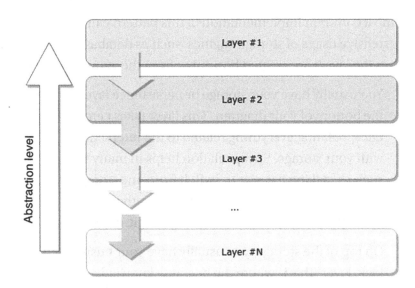

Figure 2-1. *N-layer architecture example, showing how data flows from one layer to the next*

Note   The data-flow refers specifically to the way communication is initiated, not necessarily how actual data is transmitted; otherwise, this would imply there would never be any output to the user (since any action initiated at the interface layer could never return back to it to display the result).

One common misconception about this pattern is that people confuse it with MVC (Model-View-Controller), thinking the latter to be the 3-tier version of this one. In the next pattern, I'll go over the main differences between the two.

As a side-effect of using a layered architecture, the code inside a layer is all related to the same functionality (or at least, follows a set of standards common to the rest). This in turn helps developers work independently from each other on different layers. This allows the teams to make internal changes to the layers without affecting anything else (as long as the actual interface remains the same).

21

The most common implementation of this pattern can be seen where there is extensive usage of storage engines, such as databases, because in those cases the layers are created beginning from the storage, as follows:

- You usually have your storage or persistence layer at the bottom of your diagram. This layer takes care of encapsulating everything related to the interaction with your storage. Encapsulation helps in many ways, such as making it easier to switch from one storage medium to the other, without affecting other parts of the application, such as the business logic or the UI.

- On top of the storage, you usually have your business logic layer. This is where the business knowledge resides. Whatever makes the application tick goes in here.

- Finally, on top of the previous one, you'll have your UI layer. This is the client-facing front end and the main source of interactions and data for the rest of the platform.

Some people also split the business layer into two, one in which the business knowledge remains, and another, often called the application layer, which owns the interaction logic between the UI and the business layer and also provides some common services useful for that interaction.

MVC Is Not Layered

If you've been doing any kind of web development for the last few years, you've probably heard or read about Model-View-Controller (MVC). This pattern is one that many web frameworks have adopted (Ruby on Rails, Django, and Sails.js, to name a few), because the structure of most web projects resembles this approach.

That is, in most web projects you have a UI (or View); you most likely will want to handle the requests of your UI somewhere (the Controller); and finally, you most likely have a storage engine, inside of which you can probably force your data to fit into a set of Models that represent your resources. You'll also want to perform some transformations on this.

Now, don't get me wrong; MVC is not web-specific. In fact, you can use this pattern on any application that handles some sort of domain knowledge, has a representation for it, and is capable of performing actions on it. Let me summarize what the definition says for this pattern:

- The model is the boss: here's where the domain knowledge or business logic is stored, here is where the actual data is handled, and here is where all the business specific coding should take place.

- The view is a simple representation of the model; there can even be several views for the same model. Remember that "representation" doesn't mean "web page"; it means anything that can be read and understood by another system. A JSON object can be a view; this pattern could be applied to RESTful APIs just as much as it could be implemented to the front-end architecture of your very complex SPA.

- Finally, the controller is the poor guy who drew the short stick and is in charge of interconnecting the model and the view. It basically takes input from the view and passes it along to the model, while executing whatever command is needed on that input. Then, once the controller gets something back from the model, it sends it back to the view, updating it. In some cases, the controller can even avoid the last part (as seen in Figure 2-2), letting the model directly update the view.

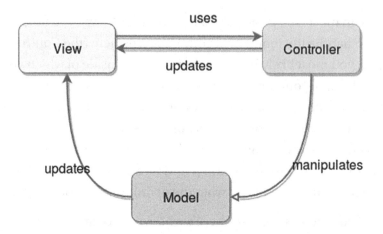

Figure 2-2. *The interaction between nodes/objects in an MVC architecture*

We now have enough information to answer the question of how this is different from a 3-layered architecture. You have seen that the layered architectural pattern does not allow jumping layers when sending messages between them. You could say that for the *n*-tier architecture, the communication is completely linear (it needs to go through all intermediate layers in all cases), while for the MVC pattern, you can work around that (as seen in Figure 2-2), since it is more of a triangular setup. This flexibility can potentially be a negative for this pattern if performance is a big concern, since every extra layer that you add to it will definitely add latency to the communication (no matter how fast you make it work).

Finally, I want to mention some of the variations on this pattern. Over the years, many adaptations have been created to improve on it, depending on whether the goal is to have less component coupling, better testing capabilities, or simply to follow a similar logic but adapted to particular needs. For instance, the MVP (Model, View, Presenter) pattern aims to remove that (normally) unwanted interaction between Model and View, making the Presenter the sole man-in-the-middle taking care of passing information between its associated View (there is only one view for each presenter) and it's Model. Another very common variation is the MVVM pattern (Model, View, ViewModel), which aims for a two-way data binding between the View and ViewModel. This in turns allows for automatic updates on the view, based on changes in the model.

Client-Server

The client-server pattern is a very simple yet powerful one. It consists of having a powerful server that provides meaningful services to many clients.

This pattern should sound very familiar to anyone who's done any web development, since it's the basic pattern for the World Wide Web. Browsers act as the many clients, which in turn request resources (web pages) from the different servers they interact with. Figure 2-3 shows what this looks like.

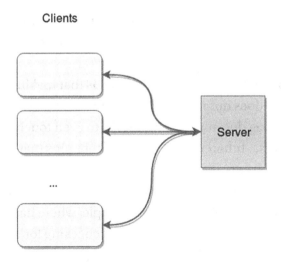

Figure 2-3. *Client-server architecture*

It's important to note two things about this pattern that you can't directly see in the diagram in Figure 2-3:

1. Clients always start the conversation. After that initial step, depending on the communication protocol/technology, the conversation between both sides might vary. For example, in HTTP the server will only be able to send back a response to specific requests from the client. If you're working with sockets, however, your server will be able to send messages to the clients that are not responses.

2. The servers are always listening for new connections from clients to start a new conversation.

This pattern favors the off-loading of application logic into the server, where more hardware resources can easily be allocated. It also keeps the clients "thin" and "dumb," in the sense that they usually don't have a lot of business logic knowledge; instead, they simply know what to request from the server, and it is in the latter where all the heavy business-related computation will take place.

One of the main benefits of this approach is that making changes and fixes to either side does not necessarily mean affecting the other. That is, fixing a server bug doesn't mean you need to even touch the client code, and vice-versa. Inherent security is another plus that comes out of this setup, since any core security check can be done on the server side, making sure any clients that are tampered with can still remain secure. (Think of a multiplayer game client, for example, where hackers can modify a player's position; if the server is still checking for that, then the modification has no effect.) The clear separation of concerns between client and server is what give you that ability.

Another benefit from thin and dumb clients is that they're easier to distribute (you don't need a 2GB client when a simple 10MB will do, and you can keep the rest of the 2GB code in the server).

Finally, consider that even though Figure 2-3 shows a single server dealing with all the clients (essentially representing a monolithic approach), your server "box" can actually be expanded into a set of microservices or any other distributed architecture you might find more useful, where there is a single point of contact between dumb clients and business logic.

In fact, if you think about it, doing that you could very well end-up with a layered pattern, in which every layer is usually a different tier (physically separated from each other). As long as your client and server layers are physically separated, your client-server architecture is essentially a 2-tier one, in which the two constraints described earlier apply.

Master-Slave

The master-slave pattern at first glance could be confused with the previous one, since it implies a single channel of communication between two parties. But conceptually they're very different, because instead of having one centralized hub for the business logic and heavy processing of data, you have a one-way controlled communication between a controlling node (the master) and many decentralized nodes (the slaves). Figure 2-4 shows an example of this architecture.

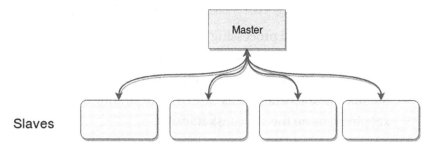

Figure 2-4. *Master-slave architecture example*

The heavy processing and expensive tasks are usually performed in the slaves, while the master merely funnels the requests from outside into them. The key aspects of this architecture are as follows:

- Any behavior-affecting messages are one-way, from the master to the slaves. Slaves don't have the ability to affect the master.

- Not all slaves need to work on the same tasks; in fact, usually this is a way to offload heavy work into multiple nodes, maintaining a single point of contact with clients of the architecture.

- Some versions of this pattern allow slaves to elect one of their own as a new master, if the current master is no longer working.

Some of the most common use cases for this pattern are:

- Database architecture. Most databases provide a version of this pattern; some of them use it to increase processing power, and others use it to provide high availability in case of a problem with their master nodes. For the latter case, slave nodes are in charge of keeping track of the master's data and staying in-sync with it to minimize the effect of a crash in the master.

- Increased parallel processing capacity. Hadoop, for example, uses a master-slave approach to dealing with its task tracker nodes. The master in this case is the JobTracker, which takes care of orchestrating and keeping tabs on the slave task trackers.

Tip   In retrospect, this pattern is one you can use to improve a
monolithic client-server architecture, by breaking up your server
into a master-slave pattern (obviously this only applies if your server
works in this way, but if you were developing a database engine, it
would be a good pattern to follow).

Event-Bus or Event-Driven Architectures

This pattern is a very interesting one in the sense that it breaks the mold
of what I've been telling you about so far. Event-driven architectures
don't have the one-to-many or many-to one type of relationship between
components; instead, they are usually many-to-many relationships. Let's
first take a look at Figure 2-5, which shows a basic example of an event-
driven architecture and then I'll go into more detail about it.

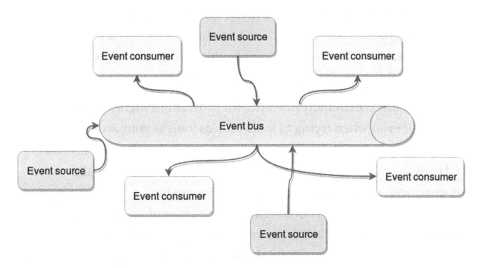

Figure 2-5. *Event-driven architecture*

The components for this architecture can be defined as follows:

- **Event sources**: These are the components that generate events and publish them into the event bus.

- **Event consumers**: The consumers are the components that are expecting a particular set of events and are ready to react to them once received.

- **Event bus**: The channel (or channels, since having multiple ones might help keep things logically separate and provide separation of concerns) through which the events will be distributed (sent from the sources to the consumers). For best results, you'll want an event bus that is capable of scaling easily and that ensures at least high availability if not fault tolerance to minimize loss of events during a problem.

- **The actual event**: Although not represented in the diagram, this is just data, in the format you want, containing the information you want. It's usually a good idea for this piece to be serializable, in order to allow it to easily be transmitted through the event bus.

This pattern is extremely powerful for providing a highly available platform, or even when trying to scale up—as long as your architecture follows the guidelines of the diagram in Figure 2-5. In other words, you need to avoid component-to-component communication and allow them to interact with each other only through the event bus.

If you do that, you can potentially replace crashed nodes with new instances in the time it takes them to boot up. The same happens if you need more processing power; you simply add new consumer or sources and connect them to the event bus, and that's all.

A good idea when dealing with this type of architecture is to use a third-party data bus (as long as that's an option), because that will allow you to focus on creating the event sources and event consumers, while at the same time using a tried-and-tested bus, one that can reliably transmit the data and scale when needed.

A classic example of this approach consists of using a message queue as the event bus. In this case you wouldn't want to create your own bus; you would most likely want to use one of the many existing solutions such as RabbitMQ, Kafka, ZeroMQ or any other.

With that being said, remember the old saying:

"With great power comes great chance of having errors."

Or something along those lines. Although this pattern might sound great, it has its limitations:

- Because of the asynchronous nature of the event bus and the event-driven reactions, your platform must also be able to function asynchronously; otherwise it will not work for you.

- Testing a logic bug on this setup is also quite challenging. You have to trace the path of the event data from one component to the other, and if the event is transformed by the actions of one of the consumers, it's even worse.

- Error handling can also be a challenge—especially if you don't standardize that across your platform.

- Another potential problem, one that is especially likely if you have a lot of components and a big team working on them, is to maintain a standard message protocol across your platform.

Microservices Architecture

This pattern is one of the best-known , since it's been growing in popularity in the last few years. Everybody and their mother is jumping into the microservices bandwagon, whether they have use for them or not. Just like with anything in our industry, there is no silver bullet solution; so hoping that microservices will solve all your problems without taking into consideration its pros and cons is reckless, at best.

The core behind this pattern is your understanding of the different features your platform is supposed to have (that is, the different services it needs to provide). If you properly understand your platform, you can probably split the services into a set of smaller services that, when used together by the client app, yield the same result you would get from a single block of code with all features bundled together. Figure 2-6 shows an example.

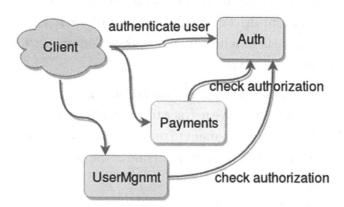

Figure 2-6. *Example of a microservices-based architecture*

By splitting your platform into individual services, you gain a new level of control over it that you never had with a monolithic approach. Figure 2-6 shows an example of a fake platform that takes care of payments. It also needs a proper authentication strategy, so it also has a dedicated Auth service. Every user needs to be authenticated against it to start using the platform, and then every request is authorized against the service. Users also have a way to register into the system, which is why there is a UserMgnmt service.

Let's assume that your site's users show the following behavior:

- They tend to use your system massively during the weekdays, but never do many payments during that time.

- On the weekends, that changes. You only get very specific traffic; not many users log-in, but the ones who do perform around 10.000 payments per second during a short period of two hours.

With a microservices-based architecture, you would:

- Gain total control over which component of your application to scale. Based on the known behavior of your customers, you could automate your platform to spawn new instances of the Auth service during the weekdays and the Payment service during the weekends.

- Improve the development process, by gaining the opportunity to create groups who can focus on each service, and develop them in parallel without affecting the rest.

- Add the ability to switch versions of your components. You could switch your Auth service; as long as you kept the same interface for it, your internal authentication logic could be completely different and no one would notice it.

- Gain the ability to reuse components or modules among applications. You could have, for example, different front ends using the same back end, selling customized versions of your application, visually tailored for your customers.

This pattern might sound like the best solution for most problems, but you need to take into account that, as with any other option, you might run into problems because you're trying to meet your needs with the wrong architecture.

Here are some of the most common issues you might run into while developing microservices:

- Communication between services needs to be properly planned; otherwise the overall performance of your system might be affected.

- Too many microservices might create a chaotic architecture. If that starts to happen, you might want to consider either a different pattern or at least some sort of orchestration service to centralize the data flow.

- Deployments of microservice-based architectures can be quite a pain, especially if you're not properly automating the process. This needs to be a high priority item in your to-do list if you're planning on going with this approach.

In the end, it'll be a matter of picking the right tool for the job, as with everything else.

The Broker Pattern

You can think of the broker pattern as a specialization of the microservices architecture. One of the pain points for the latter was that given a high enough number of microservices, you begin to need a form of orchestration; otherwise, your clients start to lose the ability to communicate easily with your platform. You start to burden them with the knowledge of where everything is in your system, and that should not be the case. Ideally, clients should be able to discover your services organically and with minimal previous knowledge.

Here is where the broker pattern comes into play. Its main component is a node called *broker,* whose purpose is to centralize and redistribute requests among different services.

Another key characteristic of this pattern is that by default it is not the broker that "knows" about its servers; instead, it's the servers that register with the broker once they come online, and provide all the information it needs to understand the services they provide.

Figure 2-7 shows an example of a broker providing services from three different servers. This pattern is very common among message queues, such as RabbitMQ,[1] Apache Kafka,[2] and Apache ActiveMQ.[3]

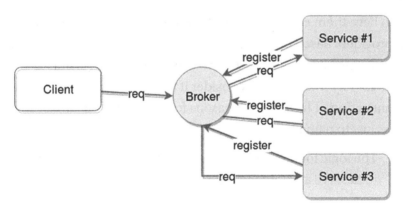

Figure 2-7. *Broker pattern showing communication between client, broker, and servers*

---

[1]See https://www.rabbitmq.com/

[2]See https://kafka.apache.org/

[3]See http://activemq.apache.org/

This pattern has a few setbacks, as they all do:

- The broker becomes the single point of failure. Or put another way, if your broker dies, you lose access to all the services it was providing.

- It's harder to scale your platform unless you also scale up your broker.

- It adds an extra layer of indirection between client and services; thus extra latency is added to the request time. This might not be a considerable increase in request time; it all depends on the type of internal logic your code will have.

The key motivation for choosing this pattern should be your need to have your clients directly connected to your service providers. If it is crucial to have them connected—perhaps because they get to choose from a set of providers based on custom criteria, or because the proximity of your servers and clients is important to you—this pattern is not for you. But it is definitely something to consider if instead you don't care about direct connection or have strong reasons for preferring the broker pattern, like these, just to name a few:

- The logic for picking the right server is complex enough to deserve a whole separate component.

- You have multiple providers of the same service, and it's not relevant who serves each request.

- You actually need physical independence between your client and servers.

Lambda Architectures

Lambda architectures are a special pattern designed to provide a high-throughput platform that is able to process very large quantities of data both in real time and in batches.

In a nutshell, processing a lot of data takes time, especially if there are complex calculations. So if your system needs to deal with those amounts of information, what ends-up happening is that either you take those calculations out and do them asynchronously, not caring how long they take (within reason obviously) and allow the users to query *those* results in real time. This provides a system that is able to properly respond to complex queries by having it all precalculated, but the downside, is that your results show a slightly old version of reality.

Alternatively, you can have a high-performant platform processing real-time data as it is received, and show those results back to the user. Again, that's great unless you need to do something that also requires the last 5 years' worth of data. Now your real-time platform is incapable of processing that amount of data properly and you have no way to give your clients the information they need.

The middle ground for this use case is where lambda architectures operate. They provide the batch-processing capabilities you require to deal with your historical information in a timely manner as well as a real-time component to process and query the latest data. Of course, your latest calculations might not be as accurate or complete as they would be if they also used the historical data, but at least you have something that will be fixed next time your batch processor runs. Figure 2-8 shows the main components of the architecture.

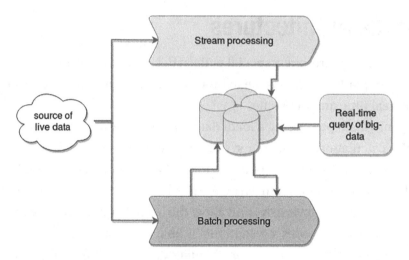

Figure 2-8. *A lambda architecture*

Given the current state of the art, some of the following products are good options for each component:

- **Batch processing**

  - Hadoop is the de facto solution for this scenario. There are multiple ways to work on top of it to process the data, such as simply working using Map/Reduce jobs, Pig,[4] or any similar batch-processing framework.

- **Stream processing**

  - Spark Streaming[5] and Apache Storm[6] are two great ways to handle this component; they both provide the speed and throughput required for stream processing tasks.

---

[4]See https://pig.apache.org/

[5]See https://spark.apache.org/streaming/

[6]See https://storm.apache.org/

- **Real time querying**

  - This component assumes the resulting outputs
    from either of the previous components still require
    special capabilities to handle. (That is, the output
    is still considered big-data, even if you're just
    querying it with a simple filter function.) Some
    good options are Apache Druid[7] and Apache
    Impala.[8]

A good example of this architecture is the way Twitter handles tweet view counts (and other stats) using a lambda approach. Twitter stores the stream of incoming events into their HDFS, and at the same time they process it using Spark Streaming. The data on the HDFS is later processed and pre-computed using a set of batch-processes which load their output into a real-time database on top of Hadoop.

Yahoo is said to also use this pattern to provide analytics on their advertising data warehouse using Apache Storm and Hadoop for real-time and batch processing of their data, while serving the end-clients through queries using Apache Druid.

With that being said, this is a solution that fits very few and specific scenarios and it's also a solution that has a very high maintenance cost associated with it since you basically are maintaining two parallel architectures at once, which in turn need to keep a centralized repository of data in a synchronized matter.

---

[7]See http://druid.io/
[8]See http://impala.apache.org/

Summary

With this chapter's abbreviated view of so many different architectural patterns I hope you've been able to see that there are many ways to solve the same problem. And ideally, you're also starting to see how some of the scaling problems mentioned in Chapter 1 can be solved using some of the patterns described here.

The next chapter will cover different ways to scale your platform, such as growing horizontally versus vertically, using load balancers, and more.

CHAPTER 3

Ways to Scale

Thus far, we've covered different architectural patterns and pain points that can cause you to want to scale your application. It is now time to start going through different scaling techniques.

This chapter will cover differences between scaling vertically and horizontally, as well as other techniques, such as using microservices, clustering, and even load balancers to handle increased traffic.

Without further ado, let's get cracking.

Scaling Techniques

It is important to note that the following techniques don't require a specific architectural pattern to be used; what I covered in the previous chapter can be considered an independent topic (in most cases) from this one. In practice, especially for big platforms with complex components, different patterns might apply depending on the needs of each one.

Vertical or Horizontal Scaling?

When it's time to start scaling, the most basic things you can do are either improving the hardware your code is running on, or simply adding more computers to distribute the load among them.

That is the essence of vertical and horizontal scaling (as seen in Figure 3-1). You can think of this as changing your old car's tires compared to buying a new Ferrari when trying to get more horsepower. With the first

© Fernando Doglio 2018
F. Doglio, *Scaling Your Node.js Apps*, https://doi.org/10.1007/978-1-4842-3991-9_3

method you're always trying to add resources to your existing hardware: memory, processing power, disk, anything that might help out depending on your needs.

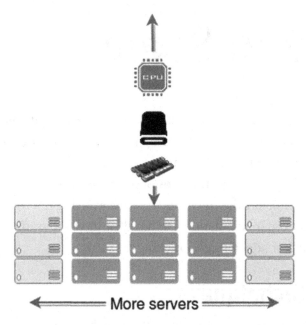

Figure 3-1. *Simple reminder diagram to understand what vertical and horizontal scaling means*

This approach normally requires some downtime because of the physical changes that need to take place. Whatever benefits you might get from doing this are limited by the resources you must add to the hardware. There is, of course, a sort of improved vertical scaling option, which is available if you're in a cloud-based environment. In these situations, your cloud provider will allow you to switch your application from one type of hardware to another. This can be done with a few clicks. Options are limited, but at least you're not constrained by your original hardware's specs. For example, Amazon will let you switch your t2.nano instance that only has half a Gigabyte worth of RAM for a t2.2xlarge one, which actually has 32 GB of RAM and 8 virtual CPUs. If memory or CPU power was your bottleneck, this would solve it).

The main problem with vertical scaling, though, is that sooner or later you're going to hit the cap for your scaling capacity. No matter what service you're paying for, eventually you'll run out of specs to improve.

And here is where horizontal scaling enters. Instead of improving a single server, you're now working with a pool of them, and adding to that pool is as simple as connecting the new server to it (or removing one from it). You can design your application to withstand such changes and avoid any real downtime when scaling. With that you gain "elasticity" in your capacity, and control over how much money you want to spend, during both normal operation and peak hours.

There are a few considerations that you should take into account when designing your architecture for horizontal scaling:

- **Service oriented architectures**: These are the easiest to horizontally scale. If yours is not designed around services, it might be a good idea to evaluate whether that pattern is a fit for your use case. As long as you have small, interconnected services, you can focus on scaling the ones that are suffering and leave the rest alone, avoiding a great deal of headaches.

- **Stateless microservices**: If your architecture is based on them, adding new copies of the services being overworked will not be a problem. I will cover this in the next chapter, but having stateful microservices keeping session information while trying to scale is not a trivial task. You will need to have extra considerations before deciding to boot-up a new copy of the affected service.

- **Tier separation**: A good idea for structuring your services is to give them a separation between their presentation, their processing, and their storage access code. This will let you focus on the main pain points. Tier separation is closely related to the previous point.

You could take it one step further even, and analyze your individual services. You could try to split them into individual components following the three-tier approach. This will give you more control over what to scale, instead of blindly scaling your entire module, because one specific part of it is affected (for example, data access inside your module might be suffering from a high workload, while the rest of it might not be as badly affected).

Taking Advantage of the Cloud

If it is elasticity you're aiming for, and your architecture is ready to be horizontally scaled, then the cloud is the right path for you. Manually handling elastic architectures is practically impossible; the main benefits of automatic elastic behavior don't usually go hand-in-hand with manual administration. For example:

- **Ability to handle highly predictable spikes of traffic with predefined growth and shrink scripts:** If you happen to have studied your traffic and have predictable patterns (that is, if you have high peaks during specific hours of the day), you can schedule your infrastructure changes. (For example, you might increase the number of processing nodes during high traffic and remove the extra ones after the peak passes.) This is a service that Azure and AWS provide, but GCP (Google Cloud Platform) doesn't, because it claims to have good enough reaction time to avoid the need for such a service.

- **Capacity to handle changes in traffic automatically with near-realtime speed**: (Note that it usually takes time to spin up new instances and scale platforms, but doing so is fast enough to be useful.) Cloud providers usually allow you to monitor different resources from your instances, such as disk space, memory, and processor utilization. You can also usually monitor custom metrics, and you can even generate them from your application to provide more accurate and precise scaling behavior.

- **Cost management**: This is another added benefit that derives from the previous points. With all cloud providers, you're always paying for what you use. So by accurately estimating the required size for your infrastructure, you gain more control over your expenses.

- **Improving the overall health of your cluster by replacing nodes that are not working correctly**: You can monitor specific indicators and decide when to terminate an unhealthy instance and replace it with a new one.

- **Better availability**: By deploying into multiple zones, you gain the ability to remain operational even when big network outages occur.

Note   In case you're not aware of the terminology, a "zone" in this scenario refers to a specific geographic location (usually a datacenter). So multi-zone deployments refer to having your code deployed in different parts of the world.

The Power of a Multi-Zone Deployment

Although it is not strictly related to scaling your architecture, taking advantage of a multi-zone deployment on the cloud is a must if you have the chance. This is usually something that most of the major cloud providers already allow, so you should consider, when planning your architecture, deploying and even scaling into multiple zones.

By doing this, you gain tolerance for big network outages that tend to affect an entire geographical zone. These types of network problems aren't very common, but when they happen, big sections of the internet are isolated from the world, and this is something you want to avoid.

There are two types of resources to consider this technique for: services and data. If it's services you're deploying, then all you have to do is make sure you're deploying behind a load balancer (such as Elastic Load Balancing for AWS). Figure 3-2 shows an example of such a case. By doing so, you've made sure that no matter what happens, your services will always be available.

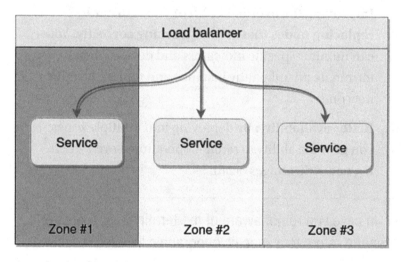

Figure 3-2. *Multi-zone service deployment*

But if you're actually deploying data, or a data storage platform such as a database, this is also a good idea for you. To make it work, however, requires some extra work. In the case of data, what you want is to make it available no matter what. To accomplish this, you must make sure you're properly replicating your data. Figure 3-3 shows one example of what such a deployment might look like.

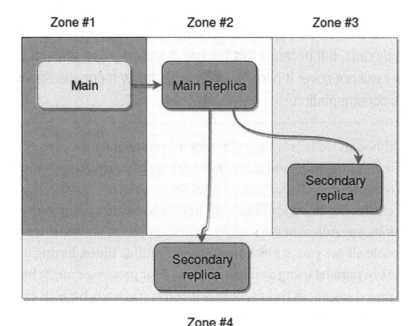

Figure 3-3. *Multi-zone replica schema*

Clustering Your Application

The term *cluster* implies a group of things acting together with a common goal; and when applied to software architecture, it usually implies a group of nodes (servers) acting together to fulfill a request.

But here I'm going to discuss clustering from a Node.js perspective and how this concept can actually help you scale your Node apps.

As you may know, Node.js runs in a single-threaded environment; and even though there may be some multi-threading involved (at the lowest levels) to help deal with asynchronous calls, that is definitely outside the normal user's realm. To all intents and purposes, Node.js is a single-threaded language, and because of that, any normal deployments will not take full advantage of your multi-core systems, unless told otherwise.

Note   Version 10.5.0 Node.js introduced experimental support for actual threads, but because this feature is still very new and not yet stable, I will not cover it here. If you want to know more, please visit Node's documentation.[1]

But although Node.js is single threaded, you still have a way to overcome this limitation and make the most out of your servers—you just need to remember to cluster your application!

The cluster module should be your first step toward scaling your applications, regardless of the scaling technique you might consider next. This module allows you to fork your process multiple times, having the forks work in parallel using as many cores as your processor might have.

The nice thing about this module is that if you already have an existing application that needs to be clustered, you don't really have to change it to make it work; you simply need to add a few lines of code and suddenly you're forking processes and having them act as a single app. Let me show you a basic example in Listing 3-1.

Tip   You don't need to download the `cluster` module from anywhere; it's included as part of the native modules in Node.

---

[1]See `https://nodejs.org/docs/latest/api/worker_threads.html`

Listing 3-1. Basic clustering example code

```
const cluster = require('cluster');
const numCPUs = require('os').cpus().length;

if (cluster.isMaster) {
  masterProcess();
} else {
  childProcess();
}

function masterProcess() {
  console.log(`Master ${process.pid} is running`);

  for (let i = 0; i < numCPUs; i++) {
    console.log(`Forking process number ${i}...`);
    cluster.fork();
  }

  process.exit();
}

function childProcess() {
  console.log(`Worker ${process.pid} started and finished`);

  process.exit();
}
```

The code from this example doesn't do much, but it is more than enough to show you how to start working with this module. And just to make sure we're all on the same page, the code in Listing 3-1 takes care of creating as many forks as there are logical cores in your CPU and inside each fork, it will print a message and then exit.

Tip   In Listing 3-1, the numCPUs variable contains the number of *logical cores* in your CPU. This means the number of physical cores times the number of threads they can handle at once. So a four-core CPU with a hyperthreading factor of 2 will have eight logical cores.

The main take-away from the example is the IF statement at the beginning of the code, because that basically implies that this file is executed at least twice: once as the main process that is executed to start the flow, and once (at least) again as the actual fork. So to avoid a classic case of the infinite forking scenario, you need that initial IF statement. The other interesting bit is that to create a new process (or worker), you simply use the cluster object and nothing else; it is completely separate from the code of the child process. This allows you to clusterize any development, new or old. Look at Listing 3-2 (the main file for a generic API based on the restify[2] module) for an example of clustering an existing API.

Listing 3-2. Example of a clusterized index.js file for a generic API

```
const restify = require("restify"),
        restifyPlugins = restify.plugins,
        config = require("config");

const cluster = require('cluster');
const numCPUs = require('os').cpus().length;

function start(){

        const server = restify.createServer(config.
        get('server'))
```

---

[2]See http://restify.com/ for more details.

```
    server.use(restifyPlugins.queryParser({
            mapParams: true
    }))
    server.use(restifyPlugins.bodyParser())

    restify.defaultResponseHeaders = data => {
      this.header('Access-Control-Allow-Origin', '*')
    }

    server.listen(config.get('server.port'), () => {
    })
}

if(cluster.isMaster) {
        for(let i = 0; i < numCPUs; i++) {
                cluster.fork();
        }
        process.exit();
} else {
        start();
}

module.exports.start = start;
```

Note   that the code in Listing 3-2 is an example from an existing project, and if you try to run it directly, without the rest of the code around it, you'll run into problems. Try to understand this code by reading it instead of by executing it.

In the example, the content for the start function is what you would normally add in your API's main file. This would start the server, set the access control headers, and configure a couple of plugins, all with the help of restify. You could very well use that code, and your entire project would work correctly. It would only take advantage of one of your CPU cores, but it would still work. But if you add the extra bits of code shown in Listing 3-2, you're now ready to start increasing your processing capacity proportionally to the number of cores in your processor. It's that easy!

The way this module works is by spawning copies of the process (by forking them) and sharing the port between them. The main worker will listen to the port you specify, and it will share the connections with the rest of the worker processes in round-robin order.

Just as when dealing with microservices and scale problems caused by in-memory session data, Node's cluster module does not provide any kind of routing logic. This means that you should not rely too much on in-memory information, since subsequent requests from the same client are not ensured to land on the same server process.

Worker processes can share information through the main process via IPC (Inter Process Communication) by using Event Emitter-like mechanics as shown in Listing 3-3.

Listing 3-3. Example of IPC used to share data through processes

```
const cluster = require('cluster');
const numCPUs = require('os').cpus().length;

if (cluster.isMaster) {
  masterProcess();
} else {
  childProcess(0);
}

function masterProcess() {
  console.log(`Master ${process.pid} is running`);
```

```
  for (let i = 0; i < numCPUs; i++) {
    cluster.fork();
  }

  for(const id in cluster.workers) {
    cluster.workers[id].on('message', msg => {
      console.log("[", msg.id,"] - ", msg.text)
    })
  }
}

function childProcess(total) {

  process.send({id: process.pid, text: `Worker ${process.pid}
executed, counter: ${total} `})
  if(total < 10) {
    setTimeout(childProcess, 1000, total + 1);
  } else {
    process.exit();
  }
}
```

This example creates one child process per core in your CPU, and each process will count from 0 to 10 at one-second intervals. On each run, a process will send its notification text to the main process through a new message broadcast using the send method of the process object.

Finally, to look at one more example, you can see in Listing 3-4 that you can't rely on in-memory data, because multiple processes might end-up handling requests.

Listing 3-4. Printing out a process ID to show how subsequent requests might yield unwanted results

```
const cluster = require('cluster');
const http = require('http');
const numCPUs = require('os').cpus().length;

if (cluster.isMaster) {
  console.log(`Master ${process.pid} is running`);

  // Fork workers.
  for (let i = 0; i < numCPUs; i++) {
    cluster.fork();
  }
} else {
  // Workers can share any TCP connection
  // In this case it is an HTTP server
  http.createServer((req, res) => {
    console.log("Worker " , process.pid, " handled the
request");
    res.writeHead(200);
    res.end('hello world\n');
  }).listen(8000);

}
```

Figure 3-4 shows the output from Listing 3-4 when a set of subsequent requests is received (as suggested by Listing 3-5). As you can see by the color-coded process IDs, not all requests will be served by the same process, which becomes a problem if you're relying on in-memory data to formulate your responses.

```
fernandodoglio@UY-IT00066 ~/workspace/personal
Master 8407 is running
Worker  8413  handled the request
Worker  8413  handled the request
Worker  8413  handled the request
Worker  8413  handled the request
Worker  8413  handled the request
Worker  8418  handled the request
Worker  8423  handled the request
Worker  8413  handled the request
Worker  8425  handled the request
Worker  8413  handled the request
Worker  8413  handled the request
Worker  8413  handled the request
Worker  8423  handled the request
```

Figure 3-4. *Output showing how requests are handled by different processes*

In order to fully test the example in Listing 3-4, you need to give your process enough traffic to merit the use of one or more cores. In my case, I used Apache Benchmark[3] to simulate 100 requests with 10 concurrent users (as seen in Listing 3-5), and the results show how throughout all of the 100 lines of output, you get the process IDs of all your instances (see Figure 3-4 for details).

Listing 3-5. Command line required to test the previous example

```
$ ab -n 100 -c 10 http://localhost:8000/
```

Clustering with PM2

The cluster module is great, because it allows you to make the most of your CPU with minimum effort; but that's about all it can do for you. If you want more control over how it's done, or need to know a bit more about what exactly is happening with your cluster, there is very little you can do out of the box.

---

[3]See https://httpd.apache.org/docs/2.4/programs/ab.html for more details.

In this case, you might want to consider an external tool such as PM2,[4] which will take care of clusterizing your app and at the same time provide monitoring and management capabilities. All you have to do is install it as shown in Listing 3-6 and then use it to start up your app (as shown in Listing 3-7).

Listing 3-6. Command line to install PM2 after you've installed Node.js

```
$ npm install pm2 -g
```

Listing 3-7. Starting your app with pm2

```
$ pm2 start index.js --name "my app" -i max
```

With that command, you'll be starting up your application, naming it "my app" in PM2's list of processes, and taking advantage of all your CPU cores (thanks to the -i max modifier). Figure 3-5 shows the output from the start command.

```
fernandodoglio@UY-IT00066 ~/workspace/personal/http-sample $ pm2 start index.js --name "my app" -i max
[PM2] Starting /home/fernandodoglio/workspace/personal/http-sample/index.js in cluster_mode (0 instance)
[PM2] Done.
```

App name	id	mode	pid	status	restart	uptime	cpu	mem	user	watching
my app	0	cluster	27226	online	0	0s	60%	33.0 MB	fernandodoglio	disabled
my app	1	cluster	27232	online	0	0s	81%	33.6 MB	fernandodoglio	disabled
my app	2	cluster	27238	online	0	0s	99%	32.1 MB	fernandodoglio	disabled
my app	3	cluster	27248	online	0	0s	80%	27.4 MB	fernandodoglio	disabled

```
Use `pm2 show <id|name>` to get more details about an app  _
```

Figure 3-5. *Output from pm2 start command*

As an added bonus, your processes are now being monitored by PM2, and if any of them crashes for any reason, it will be restarted automatically. PM2 is also saving everything you throw at stdout and stderr, so if you happen to be simply logging with console.log and console.err, you can look at that output using the command shown in Listing 3-8.

---

[4]See http://pm2.keymetrics.io/

Listing 3-8. Command to show the last few lines of the log files

```
$ pm2 logs
```

Figure 3-6 shows the possible output from the logs. As you can see, the same line is repeated four times, thanks to the four processes running in parallel (because of my four cores).

```
/home/fernandodoglio/.pm2/logs/my-app-out-1.log last 15 lines:
1|my app    | Server running at http://0.0.0.0:9000/

/home/fernandodoglio/.pm2/logs/my-app-out-0.log last 15 lines:
0|my app    | Server running at http://0.0.0.0:9000/

/home/fernandodoglio/.pm2/logs/my-app-out-3.log last 15 lines:
3|my app    | Server running at http://0.0.0.0:9000/

/home/fernandodoglio/.pm2/logs/my-app-out-2.log last 15 lines:
2|my app    | Server running at http://0.0.0.0:9000/
```

Figure 3-6. *Output from the pm2 logs command*

In Conclusion

Clustering is and should be your first step toward scaling whatever Node. js application you might be working on. Depending on your needs, you might want to go with the cluster module. You don't need anything extra; simply add a few lines of code and you're done. On the other hand, if you're looking to avoid changing your code, and you need extra support for your production environment, then PM2 or similar solutions should definitely be your choice.

Microservices to the Rescue

I've already touched on this subject during the previous chapter, and I'll probably return to it in future ones. Splitting your application into a set of services, each one small enough to be easy to maintain and focused on one or just a few functionalities, simplifies the task of scaling by replication.

In many cases horizontally scaling your application should be enough to solve whatever performance issues you might be having; but if your application is not ready for it, the cost of such a solution might end-up being too high.

Horizontal scalation means being able to both add and remove services to increase and decrease your processing power. And as you can see in Figure 3-7, doing so for a monolithic application (one that's not been properly prepared for this and has its code and logic from all services coupled) is not nearly as easy (or inexpensive) as doing it for small services within a much bigger application.

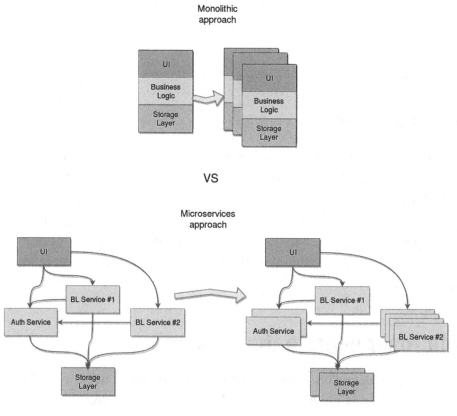

Figure 3-7. *Differences between scaling a monolithic and a microservices-based architecture*

The diagram in Figure 3-7 provides two versions of scalation by duplication. The first approach can't focus on the most affected areas, since a monolithic solution can only be considered as a unified block. Duplicating these applications is easy, because there is no inter-service communication to deal with, but the main drawback with this approach lies in the fact that if only one of your layers is affected and it's the source of your scalation needs, you still need to duplicate the entire codebase.

The second approach in the diagram, however, shows how different sections of your platform can be scaled differently depending on your needs. This is one of the many benefits provided by the microservices route (or any of its variations). That being said, you need to remember that if you're planning on doing this, you need to make sure your code is actually ready for it. The following considerations can help you in that regard:

- **Decouple your code**: This is a basic one, but if you can't follow this step, your scaling efforts are doomed. This practice will not only allow you to split your code into individual services, but it will also provide you with added benefits, such as easier-to-maintain codebase, simpler logic (which in turn usually yield fewer bugs), and added extensibility by adding new (future) services to the existing ecosystem.

- **Understand what it means to inter-communicate services**: Whether you want to accept it or not, your architecture will end-up with a (possibly) big number of services, and you need an easy way to orchestrate them and let them communicate with each other whenever necessary. I will cover this subject in the next chapter, so I'm not going to go into much detail now. That being said, you might want to think about why this subject is such a major one in scaling microservice-based architectures.

- **Automate as much as possible**: This is another item you can get away without if you're dealing with a monolithic architecture, because deploying (and other similar tasks) can be done simply by copying a set of files from one place to the other. But if you expect your platform to be easily replicated and horizontally scaled, thinking about automating deployments, having a well-defined set of coding rules and standards, and a documented control flow (such as gitflow), among other things, will definitely pay off. This is usually the case because in these type of projects several development teams need to work together, sometimes even in different code bases but creating systems that need to act as one. Once you start factoring in the human aspect of development, having a well-defined set of standards and rules definitely helps keep the chaos in check.

In Conclusion

Microservices is a topic that you'll read about throughout this book because it is a very helpful pattern for scaling Node.js platforms (since Node is usually used to create APIs).

That being said, and as I've already covered in previous chapters, it is not a silver bullet and will not work for you every time. You need to remember when this pattern is helpful and how you need to prepare your code and your team to be able to get the most out of it.

Summary

There is no one way to scale your architecture; in fact, there is even more than one way to cluster your Node.js applications. In this chapter I've tried to show you a few ideas about how to tackle this topic; it is up to you to apply them to your own circumstances.

In the next chapter, I'll cover some common problems that arise when starting to scale your application for the first time and offer some suggestions for tackling them.

CHAPTER 4

Challenges when Scaling

When scaling your platform or adapting it to allow scaling, you will usually run into problems or challenges you didn't have with your older version. This should not stop you from trying, as these challenges are inherent from the added complexity of your new design.

They're sometimes related to secondary subsystems, the ones that aren't strictly working toward getting the business rules to work, but instead address issues such as where you store your log files. And sometimes the challenges actually affect more important aspects of your application, such as the data you keep in-memory and how to translate that into a multi-node scenario.

In this chapter, I'll cover the major hurdles you might find during your scaling endeavors and how you can overcome them.

Dealing with Your Log Files

Paying attention to your logging strategy from the beginning of your project is often a good idea; otherwise, you may run into problems. This might sound like an empty warning, but take a step back from your code, and think about how you're logging right now and what you're doing with that information.

© Fernando Doglio 2018
F. Doglio, *Scaling Your Node.js Apps*, https://doi.org/10.1007/978-1-4842-3991-9_4

If you don't really have a use for it, then you might as well stop logging, but if you're actually getting insights from the data, either when troubleshooting, or through some sort of analytics tools, then make sure you can keep doing so after you've scaled up (or down) your architecture. Can you trust that you will be able to process your logging data if you're under an elastic scaling architecture?

Our end-goal when it comes to dealing with logs is depicted in Figure 4-1, where you can see multiple instances of several different services sending their logging messages to a centralized system. This system can be either an in-house cluster or a third party service (such as Splunk,[1] Loggly,[2] or Logz.io,[3] to name just a few). Note that it should be a cluster or something capable of scaling like one, because it will need to keep up with your architecture.

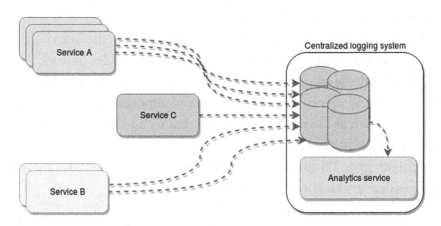

Figure 4-1. *Example of a centralized logging architecture, where multiple instances of different services are sending their logging information into a single system*

---

[1]See https://www.splunk.com/ for more details.
[2]See https://www.loggly.com/ for more details.
[3]See https://logz.io/ for more details.

The way these services send their data to their destination will vary depending on the nature of that system, but usually standard ways will be provided (the most common ones are either RESTful APIs or agents you can install on your servers and configure to send the data to a remote location by themselves).

There are two very common mistakes developers make when logging in new systems that aren't necessarily hard to fix, but require attention when scaling. The first mistake is logging only into `stdout` and `stderr`; the second is logging into a single file. These issues will need to be addressed if we want to get anywhere near the ideal scenario of Figure 4-1.

You're Just Logging into stdout and stderr

And what makes it even worse is that you're not wrapping the output function/method of your language of choice into a construct under your control. In other words, and in the Node.js universe, you're logging using `console.log` and `console.error`.

This is great for small projects and quick PoC (Proof of Concept), but if you're interested in getting anything out of your logs, then you need to do something about it. In particular, because both the `stdout` and `stderr` are local to each server instance, if you start scaling your application into multiple servers, you'll have to deal with distributed logs that aren't being saved anywhere (or maybe they are, depending on your setup).

Fortunately, there are several ways to solve this, again depending on where you're currently standing. For instance, if you're using PM2 or something like it, you'll get access to the logs for all instances of your process within the same server (see Chapter 3 for more details on PM2), simply by running the following command:

```
$ pm2 logs
```

This will work, even if you're not saving the data anywhere, since PM2 will catch all your output and save it automatically, just in case. But that will only get you halfway, since we also need to send those log files into a centralized location.

Because there are so many options, and so many variations of similar solutions, I'm just going to cover a simple one, assuming you have an ELK[4] (Elastic, Logstash, and Kibana) cluster configured and ready to receive logs somewhere on your architecture. This will act as the centralized logging and analytics system from Figure 4-1.

What you want to do in this situation is configure something that will ship the log files stored by PM2, into Logstash, which in turn will apply any transformation you might need to the data and then send it and index it into Elastic for your consumption using Kibana.

This might sound like a lot at first glance, especially if this is your first time dealing with something like this, but it is a scalable way of going about it. If you do it right, you gain the ability to support failures and downtimes on your Elastic cluster, you get back-pressure, on your ogging pipeline, making sure you're not overwhelming your analytics platform, and so on.

To achieve this, you'll install and configure Filebeat in all your servers (all those that need to send data out). Filebeat is essentially a log shipper that follows a standard protocol called Beat. This shipper (and its associated protocol) is the result of several years of iteration by the team of Elastic to get the best and most lightweight log shipper possible.

To install it, you can download it from the official website[5] and then to configure it, you can edit the `filebeat.yml` file (which will be located in its installation folder, in my case, it was in `/etc/filebeat`), making it look like Listing 4-1.

---

[4]See `https://www.elastic.co/elk-stack` for more details.

[5]You can download it from `https://www.elastic.co/downloads/beats/filebeat`.

Listing 4-1. Configuration content to make `filebeat` send the logged data into logstash

```
filebeat.prospectors:
- input_type: log
  paths:
        - [YOURHOMEFOLDER]/.pm2/logs/yourapp*.log

document_type: yourapp-name
fields_under_root: true

output.logstash:
  hosts: ["LOGSTASH-HOST:5044"]
```

That configuration will pull the contents of the log files for your app (stored in a default location by PM2) and into a Logstash server. You need to replace the constants YOURHOMEFOLDER and LOGSTASH-HOST by the actual values to make it work.

With that, you can start the shipper in daemon form using the command from Listing 4-2.

Listing 4-2. Execution of `filebeat`

```
$ sudo filebeat  -e -c /etc/filebeat/filebeat.yml
```

Tip I recommend making sure that line runs every time your server starts; otherwise, you'll stop sending data after the first server reboot.

With that, you're ready to retrieve your log files (if you're crazy enough to log using only console.log). But you still need to configure Logstash to make sure you can parse these logs, transform them (if needed) and then index them into Elastic. So stop smiling, and keep reading.

Assuming you've already installed your Logstash server, you need to configure it to use the Filebeat plugin and output that data into Elastic. In other words, you need to create a configuration file that looks like Listing 4-3.

Listing 4-3. Configuration file (any file with a .conf extension) for Logstash

```
input {
  beats {
    port => 5044
  }
}

output {
  elasticsearch { hosts => ["ELASTIC-HOST:9200"] }
  }
```

Note that the configuration from Listing 4-3 will only receive and index data; it will not transform (which is one of the key benefits of Logstash) anything. So if you wanted to do some extra tweaking of your logs before indexing them, I recommend looking at the full documentation for Logstash.[6] Also, make sure to match the port under the configuration for the Beat plugin with the port specified on the Filebeat config file (Listing 4-1).

You're now set. Congratulations, you've managed to avoid a major problem by using the right set of tools.

---

[6]See https://www.elastic.co/guide/en/logstash/current/configuration.html for more details about configuring Logstash.

Note   Even if you have some form of workaround in place to centralize your logs, using `console.log` and `console.error` for logging purposes is far from ideal. Creating a simple wrapper around these methods (at the very least) will grant you more control over the log formats, extra information you might want to add, and so on.

If, on the other hand, you weren't using anything like PM2 that would catch the output of your process and save it into a file, you're out of luck. You've lost your logs to the black hole that lives inside every server and there is no way for you to retrieve them. So don't do it like this.

You're Logging into a Single File

This is a better scenario than the previous one, even though it's still far from ideal. You're now correctly wrapping your output function/method with something you can control (that is, you have your own logger). You're even saving that information into a log file, which is great, but because you're not in control over what, where, and when you log, you need to consider other things, like the following:

- **File size**: How much space can you allocate to your logs? Are you sure you're not depleting your hard disk, causing your application to possibly fail due to lack of space?

- **History**: How much history do you want to keep in your file? This will depend on your application logging needs. If you need to keep a lot of debugging information in your files, then a lot of history is not recommended, since you'd end-up with huge files. On the other hand, if you're not logging a lot of events, you might as well keep as much as you can (always taking into account the previous point).

You could potentially take care of both from inside your own code, by adding extra logic to your logger and make sure you properly keep the size and history of your logs in check. You can also use an external tool, such as the classic logrotate[7] command line utility, which is already part of most (if not all) Linux distributions.

In order to use this utility to solve your problems, you'll have to create a configuration file, something that looks like Listing 4-4.

Listing 4-4. Configuration file required to rotate sample log file

```
/your/app/path/logfile.log {
        compress
        rotate 5
        size 300M
}
```

With that configuration, your log file will be rotated whenever it reaches 300 MB in size, and after the fifth rotation, that file will be removed (in other words, history is kept up to five rotations). You can now execute logrotate specifying the path to the new configuration file, as shown in Listing 4-5.

Listing 4-5. Executing logrotate

```
$ logrotate /path/to/your-new-configuration-file.conf
```

This is definitely the preferred way of handling this logic instead of writing it directly into your own logger's code. But you're not there yet. You now have your own log file, and you're properly making sure it doesn't grow out of hand, but you still need to send its content into a centralized location. You can look at the previous point in order to understand how to configure Filebeat and Logstash.

---

[7]See https://linux.die.net/man/8/logrotate for more details.

With that last bit of configuration, you're ready to move on with your development, because you again have a stable logging system within your platform.

Throw Away Your Logger and Use a Real One

There is yet another way of solving this problem. Instead of using an external tool to solve it, use the right logging module in your system. This solution applies to any type of system, and in most cases I recommend it over building your own custom tool.

The one logging module I always recommend and tend to use, thanks to the flexibility it provides, is Winston.[8] Currently on version 3.0.0, it provides the developer with all the tools needed to create a scalable and professional logger that will allow you to reach your end-goal with a minimum of effort.

It is not unique in many of its features, but it's definitely one of the most common ones, which makes it the usual target for others to contribute to. This in turn, helps because thanks to that fact, it has over 20 different "transports" already developed. They will help you integrate your logger with external systems out of the box.

Look at the example in Listing 4-6, which was taken almost entirely from Winston's documentation.

Listing 4-6. Basic winston-based custom logger

```
const winston = require("winston");

const logger = winston.createLogger({
  level: 'info',
  format: winston.format.json(),
  transports: [
```

---

[8]See https://www.npmjs.com/package/winston for details on the module.

```
    new winston.transports.File({ filename: 'error.log', level:
    'error' }),
    new winston.transports.File({ filename: 'combined.log' })
  ]
});

if (process.env.NODE_ENV !== 'production') {
  logger.add(new winston.transports.Console({
    format: winston.format.simple()
  }));
}
```

In this example, you can see that we have two different transports (although they're both files, they're different ones), one for error events and the other for everything (including errors). Then, for production-only environments, it will also log into stdout (the console).

It is not very difficult to turn that code into something that's compatible with the ELK stack from before; simply add a new transport and that's it. Look at Listing 4-7 to see how it would look).

Listing 4-7. Modified logger ready to index data into Elastic

```
const winston = require("winston");
const ES = require("winston-elasticsearch");

const logger = winston.createLogger({
  level: 'info',
  format: winston.format.json(),
  transports: [
    new winston.transports.File({ filename: 'error.log', level:
    'error' }),
```

```
  new winston.transports.File({ filename: 'combined.log' }),
  new ES({level: 'info'})
  ]
});

if (process.env.NODE_ENV !== 'production') {
  logger.add(new winston.transports.Console({
    format: winston.format.simple()
  }));
}
```

With a few added lines and a new transport, you're now ready to index your logs into Elastic, which in turn, will be consumed by Kibana for your log analytics.

Tip   Note how this approach actually avoids using Logstash altogether and indexes data directly into Elastic. But there are also several benefits of going through Logstash, and for that, you can use the `winston-logstash`[9] module.

Sharing Memory between Processes

Let's forget about log files for now and think about something a bit more complicated. Sharing memory between two or more processes might be problematic when scaling because if you're already trying to share data while clustering (between master and workers) or you're thinking about starting to communicate two or more processes through memory, then you have to start thinking in a distributed fashion.

---

[9]See `https://www.npmjs.com/package/winston-logstash` for more details.

When scaling, you will start running into multi-server scenarios, and by default your servers don't share memory. You have to stop thinking about sharing variables and memory space and start thinking about exteriorizing that shared data and moving it into outside storage.

If you're using shared memory, I'm assuming that performance and read speed are a concern, so moving this data into any type of storage is not an option; we need something that will provide the same type of performance gain (or as close as possible) with minimal integration effort. You will have to restructure your code if you're already doing that; there is no way around this, but at least we can try to minimize the damage.

There is no better way to move away from sharing memory and into a shared memory between your processes than choosing one of the many options, such as Redis[10] (a complex key-value, in-memory storage system, with support for complex data structures, pub/sub and other useful features), Memcached[11] (a simplified version of Redis, with a multithreaded architecture), AWS ElastiCache[12] (which essentially is a managed version of the first two), and so on.

The ideal goal (is to achieve something similar to what is shown in Figure 4-2.

---

[10]See http://redis.io for more details.

[11]See https://memcached.org for more details.

[12]Read more about ElastiCache here https://aws.amazon.com/elasticache/.

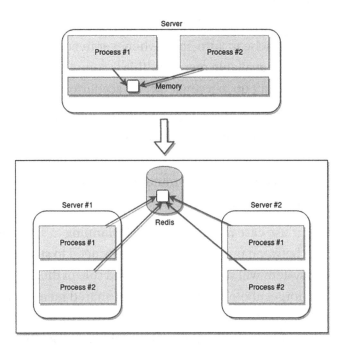

Figure 4-2. *Migration from sharing memory between processes into an external shared memory system*

All of the technologies mentioned are essentially in-memory databases. They all allow you to store small bits of information (strings, objects, numbers, basically anything you can put in a basic variable and in some cases, a bit more) and share it with other processes. With this approach, you get several benefits over simply sharing memory:

- Support for multi-server scenarios, where they can all access the same information, no matter where it came from.

- Stable and reliable in-memory storage, which you can use to centralize the shared information. These systems are developed to be resilient and in most cases, they allow for high availability or fault tolerance support.

- Unlimited memory to share data. You can setup AWS EastiCache to auto-scale whenever needed and increase the available memory. This is something you definitely can't do in a single-server scenario.

- Depending on your use case and your choice, you might even get extra benefits, such as the Redis pub/sub or keyspace notifications, which allow you to work reactively with in-memory mutations (such as changes in a value, or additions to a list).

Whatever your use case might be, if you're planning to share or already sharing memory between processes and you now need to start thinking about how your system will scale up, then a good rule of thumb is to go higher-level and forget about it. Just extract that shared memory into an in-memory database that you can manage (or have managed for you). They are less complicated to maintain and provide far more benefits at a very high access speed. And yes, I understand that they can't match the read speed of shared memory, but once again, you should double-check your needs based on your use case and think long and hard about whether the added performance of that setup is actually worth the limitations and complications it also brings with it.

Single Points of Failure? No Thank You!

It may seem obvious, but you should avoid having single points of failure (SPOFs) whenever possible. They are basically your weakest link and if they break, your entire application/platform/system will be rendered useless.

That being said, they also have the habit of sneaking into some architectures when you're not looking for them. This is especially true when systems start growing organically instead of systematically, and you start adding new bits and pieces based on your most recent needs, without thinking about the future. For example, without going too far from what we've been talk about, imagine having to start sharing memory between processes. You've followed my earlier advice, but miss the very crucial part about setting up your external memory in cluster mode, so you end up with something that looks like Figure 4-3.

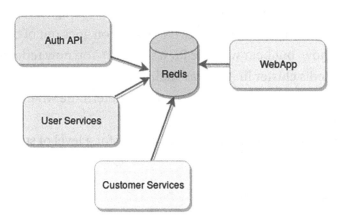

Figure 4-3. *Redis as a single point of failure*

In this scenario, all services depend on Redis, but Redis is not set up to be able to handle any type of problems; in fact, there is only one instance of Redis running. If it fails, your entire system will be rendered useless. The fix for this one is easy enough; just change the way you have your Redis running. You'd probably set it up as a cluster, or with Sentinel,[13] so your master nodes will have a slave assigned just in case.

Getting rid of single points of failure can be as easy as setting up a cluster or as hard as adding redundancy to your entire platform. It mostly depends on how far you can take the process until it no longer provides enough bang for your buck.

---

[13]Read https://redis.io/topics/sentinel for more details.

Let me give you another example, going back to Figure 4-3. After you set up your minimum Redis cluster (which by definition will already contain three master nodes and three slave nodes) you realize that all nodes could fail, because they're servers you actually have inside your own datacenter. So you decide to move to the cloud and deploy your own Redis cluster in AWS. You then realize that all those servers could still be unreachable if there is a region-level outage, so you again redeploy on a multi-region setup. Great, but what if Amazon goes out of business (unlikely, I know, but bear with me for a second)? You now redeploy your multi-zone Redis cluster in Azure as well, and you have both multi-zone load balancers and extra logic in your code to determine when to pick each one.

You're now paying a whole lot more money for a level of stability that you might never need.

Knowing When to Stop

Understanding that you have SPOFs is half the battle; knowing when to stop going down the rabbit hole is the other half. I've had discussions with teammates who argued that my managed Redis cluster was a SPOF because most of my services actually needed it for some task (Figure 4-3 is based on personal experience). It can definitely be a chokepoint if it's not properly optimized, but given our use case and business needs, it made no sense to even start thinking about contingencies if that cluster were to fail, because if it did, a lot of other things would also fail and honestly, our SLAs did not cover that much availability.

So when do you stop and say: "this is good enough"? In my opinion a good tool for that is the SLA (Service Level Agreement) you sign with your users or clients regarding the performance, availability, and overall quality of your service. It usually boils down to a number, a percentage that is between 90% and 100% (such as 99%, also known as "two nines," or 99.99%, known as "four nines") and is in the context of a period of time (the most common ones are a week, a month, or even a year).

You basically take that percentage from the number of minutes in the time period defined, and you have how much uptime your system is expected to have in that timeframe. But reaching that number is not an act of magic or pure guesstimation; it's a process that if done correctly, requires a lot of analysis and discussion.

To give you a quick overview (you should dig deeper into this subject if you're not familiar with the concepts that are coming), the tools you'll need to properly find that number are called system-level indicators (SLIs) and system-level objectives (SLOs).

System-Level Indicators (SLIs)

These are metrics you will develop and measure constantly to understand how your system is performing. They are not strictly hardware- or performance-related; they are business-related. In some cases they might be obvious, such as counting how many web pages load within an acceptable timeframe (100ms, for example) on web apps. But in others they might not be, such as comparing the number of billing requests in your web-server log files against your database records at the end of the day and making sure the percentage of correlation is close to 100%. These indicators should be set based on conversations between developers, devops/sysadmins or whatever flavor of them you have on your team, and the business.

All three parts of the equation must be present and must give their opinion as to what makes an indicator relevant and measurable. Each SLI should have a basic description of what it's meant to measure from a business perspective and then a detailed description of how it needs to be measured from a technical perspective. Basically, the more documentation you can write about an SLI, the easier it will be to both maintain it and review it in future iterations.

To define your SLIs properly, remember to keep them user-centric (it might be a good idea to define them based on the user journeys for your application) and to think about metrics that can be measured in the form of "good events" divided by the "total number of events" times 100. This will provide metrics like "proportion of home page requests loading in under 100 ms."

There are some predefined SLI types that might come in handy to guide you while defining your own; they are related to the type of subsystem you're trying to analyze, for example:

- If you have a user-facing section of your application, you might want to think of using SLIs of the availability, latency and throughput types. Or put another way, you want SLIs that ask, "can my system provide a response to a request?," "how long does it take to do it?," and "how many requests can it handle?"

- on The other hand, if you have a storage system you want to keep track of, you might want to consider going with latency, availability, and durability SLIs. These ask, "How long does it take to read and write?," "can we actually request data from it?," and "is the data there if we need it?"

- Finally, Big Data projects have specific types as well, such as throughput and end-to-end latency. For instance, you can ask things like "how much data are we processing?" and "how much time does data need to go from ingestion to final storage?"

System Level Objectives (SLOs)

These are the objectives you want to aim for on each of your indicators. They're percentage numbers in a timeframe, just like the SLAs, but internal. They're not shared with your users or customers, since they usually act as the upper limit of what you expect your system to do, not exactly what you want to state that your system *can* do to the outside world. (In other words, try not to shoot yourself in the foot by sharing these values.)

You should arrive at them based on your understanding of your user's needs, which is why having the business represented in these meetings is important. Sometimes techies like the developers or the sysadmins will only think from their technical expert positions and forget about what the user actually feels like and wants from the application they're building. This is not to say they shouldn't help define the objectives, which must be a group effort to avoid leaving anything out.

These defined objectives are crucial because in the context of rooting out SPOFs, you need them to understand when to stop pursuing that goal and start shipping.

When it comes to the number of SLIs and SLOs to write, as a rule you can probably assume one SLO per SLI and up to three SLIs per user journey. If you start seeing a lot of relevant SLIs being defined as a result of these meetings, you should consider grouping them into more generic topics. For example, if you happen to have three or four different SLIs that talk about loading time of web pages, you can probably collapse them all into a generic one that's not related to a single user journey but to several (or maybe all of them).

What Happens When We Don't Meet Our SLOs?

Finally, and although it's not entirely related to SPOFs, if we're talking about SLIs and SLOs, we need to understand what to do when those numbers aren't met. Because you can identify your key user journeys and create all the SLIs you want for them, and you can sit down for weeks with the business, your devops, and your developers and come up with realistic and reachable SLOs for those indictors. But you also have to expect the system to fail at some point and not meet those numbers.

When that happens, you should already have a plan for it in your deployment and development policies. You should be keeping track of the failures and count the time your system is not conforming as expected. If this time exceeds a given preset amount (some people call it an *error budget*), then you need to have already defined what to do. For example, you may decide to hold back work on new features until major bugs are fixed, or cancel new deployments until bugs causing the issues are found and fixed. These are all strategies you need to think about while working on your indicators and objectives.

Agreeing on Your SLAs

The final step in this process will be agreeing on your SLAs, which obviously will depend on your business case and use cases, but should be kept under the objectives, with the intent of preventing your user from expecting excellence in a scenario where not everything is 100% up to you and your team. Service providers might fail to deliver, and even if you don't, your users will fault you and see your services as the one not fulfilling the predefined agreement.

Stateful Apps and Multi-Server Scenarios

Last but certainly not least is the problem that we might run into in systems that store in-memory information about active user sessions. When this happens and we start duplicating these services into multi-server scenarios, the usual setup includes a load balancer in front of all these new servers. This load balancer will in turn distribute the load as equally among all servers as possible, and there is no guarantee that your user will land two subsequent requests on the same server.

Figure 4-4 shows exactly this scenario, with the end-result of having a partial fragment of your user session in each receiving server.

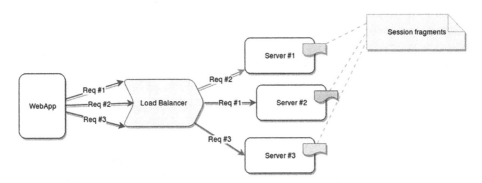

Figure 4-4. *Example of a web application making three requests for the same user and landing on three different servers*

This is far from ideal, and it can cause some serious issues if your servers' logic depends on that information. The good news, though, is that this is relatively easy to fix, and in some cases, it will not even require any code changes.

The first and obvious fix for this scenario, is, as I've already covered in this chapter, to remove the in-memory information from the server and move it into an external storage, such as Redis. This would, of course, involve code changes and the added complexity of setting up and maintaining the Redis cluster. The upside is that it doesn't affect the balancing strategy used by your load balancer and helps keep your load evenly distributed.

Figure 4-5 shows how this solution would end-up looking. Requests would still be randomly hitting each server (which is ideal), but the session information is centralized in the external memory; that is, Redis.

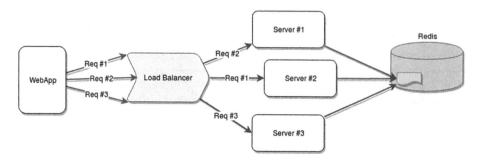

Figure 4-5. *Solving the fragmented session problem using external memory access*

That solution however, involves possibly quite a lot of code changes, since your entire server could be stateful and depend heavily on in-memory user state information. If that is too big a change right now, and your team or project can't really afford it, you will have to consider configuring your load balancer to handle sticky sessions. Figure 4-6 shows how this solution would look.

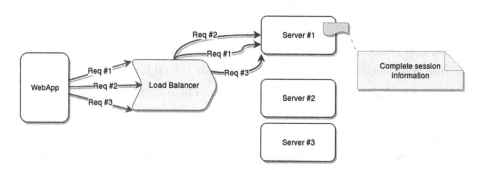

Figure 4-6. *Solving the fragmented session problem with sticky sessions*

Sticky sessions is the term for a method used by some load balancers and routers to link a specific user to one of their balanced servers based on information contained in the HTTP requests sent. Once that link is made, every subsequent request that can be identified as coming from the same client will land on the same server. This solves the problem you were having, and configuring your classic load balancers fort this behavior is not difficult at all. For example, Listing 4-8 shows how to configure Apache using the mod_proxy_balancer[14] module to handle sticky sessions.

Listing 4-8. Example of Apache configuration to handle sticky sessions

```
Header add Set-Cookie "ROUTEID=.%{BALANCER_WORKER_ROUTE}e;
path=/" env=BALANCER_ROUTE_CHANGED
<Proxy "balancer://mycluster">
    BalancerMember "http://192.168.1.50:80" route=1
    BalancerMember "http://192.168.1.51:80" route=2
    ProxySet stickysession=ROUTEID
</Proxy>
ProxyPass        "/test" "balancer://mycluster"
ProxyPassReverse "/test" "balancer://mycluster"
```

Most of the common load balancers already have support for this feature, but you have to make sure it makes sense on your side to have it as well, since it could cause some difficulties if you start using HTTPS; because request information can't be analyzed, other methods need to be used to identify requests. You might also run into unbalanced servers receiving too much traffic, just to name a couple of possible issues.

In the end, this technique is just as valid as turning your stateful services into stateless ones; you just need to make sure that by going this way, you're not hiding design flaws on your code.

---

[14]See https://httpd.apache.org/docs/2.4/mod/mod_proxy_balancer.html for more details.

Summary

That is it for problems that can arise when scaling your system. My intention wasn't to scare you away from attempting to scale; it was to give you the tools that you might need to solve those problems should they happen to you.

In the next chapter I'm going to cover how to monitor your platform in order to understand when to scale up or down. This is something that can be done both reactively and proactively, but you have to understand how your platform behaves before deciding on a strategy.

CHAPTER 5

When to Scale?

Having the tools to scale your architecture but lacking the data to understand when to use them is like having the keys to your dream car but not knowing how to drive it. You need the information to back up your scaling decisions. You need to understand when your inbound traffic is too big for a single server, or when your database processor is screaming in pain asking for a sibling to help take the load off.

In this chapter I'm going to cover some of the most common tools that will enable you to both monitor different key aspects of your platform and react to those results by triggering an elastic behavior in your platform.

Monitoring

There are different ways to monitor your application or platform. As you can see in Figure 5-1, at the lowest level you can look into infrastructure monitoring, where you can keep track of things like CPU usage, free memory, and disk space utilization. You can do that on your own servers (where your app is deployed) or in your related services' servers (such as database servers, CDN servers, and others).

© Fernando Doglio 2018
F. Doglio, *Scaling Your Node.js Apps*, https://doi.org/10.1007/978-1-4842-3991-9_5

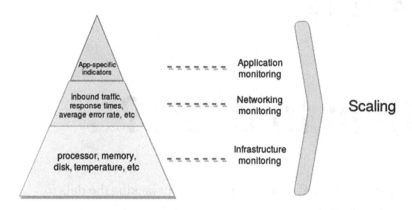

Figure 5-1. *Different types of monitoring*

If you go one level up, you can start monitoring your networking devices, such as load balancers, routers, and others. From them, you can get information related to the traffic your app is getting, and you can also get some level of details about response codes to understand what kind of problems you might be dealing with. The information you'll get at this level will be domain-specific, and you'll need to have some basic level of understanding about the app you're trying to monitor to understand how to respond to this information (unlike monitoring CPU load or disk space utilization, where no matter what you're doing, no disk space is always bad).

Finally, the top layer is reserved for app-specific indicators. These are the ones you can't just "pull" from places; you have to first put them there by writing the required code. These are hyper-specific indicators that are only relevant to your use case and make sense only within the business rules of your application. Depending on the type of monitoring system you might be using, you could simply need to add this ad-hoc information into your log messages and then by parsing that data, you'll get the indicators. Or you could also be using some third-party module to send those new indicators into your monitoring system directly.

Whatever your application might be, if you're worried about your scaling needs, it might be a good idea to start from the bottom and move up as your architecture grows. Many systems are great with basic infrastructure monitoring, but the more complex the app (meaning, the logic rules behind it), the higher up you'll have to go on the pyramid.

Alerting

A final concept for monitoring in general, before we start delving deeper into each of the levels I just mentioned, is *alerting*. This can mean anything; it can be sending an email to the user or it can be notifying some system that can it perform predefined actions. Whatever it might mean to you, it's the whole point of this practice: you monitor and then you react to the values received.

Deciding when to send those alerts is also very important; both the triggering condition and the periodicity of the messages need to be taken into account to provide a good user experience and add value. Alerting for the sake of alerting is the worst thing you can do; the only thing you'll achieve by doing that is overwhelming your users to the point where received alerts will be ignored.

Instead of that, you should create a custom alerting strategy for your platform, one that takes into account your domain knowledge and acts accordingly. Some suggestions:

- **Use different alerting channels**: Depending on the severity and importance of what you're alerting about, you might want to send that alert via email if it's something your user should look at in the next few hours. You might want to simply send an in-app notification or leave some sort of alerting record if it's something that needs to be reviewed eventually; or you can send a page, an SMS, or even a WhatsApp message to your user's phone if the alert is really critical and she should take a look immediately.

- **Try to alert on symptoms instead of specific problems**: For example, alerting when your homepage is taking too long to load is a symptom, which might be caused by various specific problems such as your database server being overloaded, your Redis cluster failing, or your web server's disk running out of space, to name a few. When you alert on symptoms, you're providing context to your users, letting them know how the current problem is affecting your customers. As an added bonus, your alerts aren't bound to your infrastructure. Going back to the previous example, suppose you were to remove your Redis cluster because you no longer needed it, and instead added an Elastic instance into the mix. If you were alerting on symptoms, your users will still be getting the same alerts when problems with Elastic start causing delays on the homepage loading times; but if you weren't, then you now have to introduce visible changes by removing old alerts (the ones related to Redis) and new ones (for Elastic). In other words, your alerts are more durable if they're based on symptoms.

- **Try to alert only when the problems are real**: This might be an understatement, but your alerting strategy should be smart enough to understand when the symptoms being reported are due to an actual problem and when they're caused by a known maintenance window (for example). A planned server update might overload your processors for a few hours, causing some slow response times on your platform, but you definitely don't want to wake up your sysadmin at 3 a.m. because of that.

- **Make sure your alerting strategy allows you to be proactive and not reactive to your problems**: There is a very big difference between being notified when your system is taking 300ms longer to load than normal and being notified when your pages aren't loading at all. You obviously want the second kind of alert (you should always prepare for the worst), but it shouldn't be the only one.

Monitoring Your Apps

Specifically when it comes to monitoring Node.js applications, there are too many possibilities to cover them all in this book, and eventually we would start seeing repeated features. And we're not just looking for a monitoring tool, remember that we're trying to set up an environment that can scale up and down, according to our needs. So we need a solution that can monitor and react to the values receive by triggering a set of scaling rules.

So instead of reviewing products such as PM2 Enterprise,[1] or even Prometheus,[2] I'm going to review how to set up AWS CloudWatch[3] to monitor your application and your infrastructure at the same time (so you'll be able to cover the entire pyramid from Figure 5-1) and on top of that, how to make it react and trigger new instances of your application. Figure 5-2 shows the base architecture we'll use for this example.

---

[1]See `https://pm2.io/enterprise` for more details.

[2]See `https://prometheus.io/` for more details.

[3]See `https://aws.amazon.com/cloudwatch` to learn more.

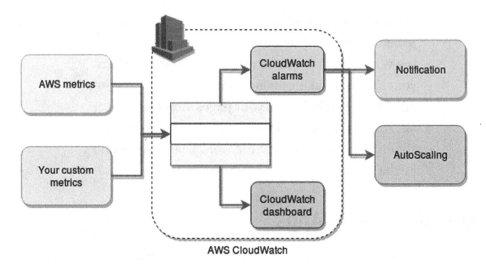

Figure 5-2. *Monitoring/Alerting/Scaling diagram using AWS*

The idea behind this example is that CloudWatch will be gathering metrics both from our own application (ad-hoc metrics) and from AWS services that already provide them automatically (such as EC2). These metrics will be monitored by AWS CloudWatch Alerts and displayed and charted by AWS CloudWatch Dashboard. The alerts will trigger actions, which can be anything ranging from a notification (via email, SMS, or even an SQS queue) to a call to the AWS AutoScaling service.

In order to look at this, we'll use a sample application, so you can see how the ad-hoc metrics can be provided to AWS using their own libraries. This sample app is going to be mind-numbingly simple, but the point is to avoid distracting you by looking at unimportant code, so bear with me.

The code from Listing 5-1 is simply an API endpoint that will return the current time every time you send a request to it. The only dependency this code has is the ExpressJS library, and I'm going to assume you already know how to install that one.

Listing 5-1. Code for "What's the time?" API

```
const express = require('express')
const app = express()

app.get('/', (req, res) => res.send(Date()))

app.listen(3000, () => console.log("What's the time API up and
running on port 3000"))
```

To start the refactoring process, we'll begin by installing the SDK module from AWS, and with it, we'll create a basic metric reporter, which will let us send custom metrics back to CloudWatch.

Listing 5-2 show how to install this new module; make sure you add the --save flag to it, to ensure that the dependency is saved into your package.json file.

Listing 5-2. Installation of AWS's SDK module

```
$ npm install aws-sdk --save
```

After the installation is complete, we can begin to send custom metrics using the putMetricData method provided by the library. This method takes two parameters, a JSON object with the metrics to send, and a callback. Clearly the interesting parameter here is the first one, so let's go over its structure in Listing 5-3.

Listing 5-3. Structure and data type of the metrics parameter

```
{
  MetricData: [
    {
      MetricName: String,
      Dimensions: [
        {
```

```
            Name: String,
            Value: String,
          }
       ],
       StatisticValues: {
          Maximum: Float,
          Minimum: Float,
          SampleCount: Float,
          Sum: Float
       },
       StorageResolution: Int,
       Timestamp: Date or String or Int,
       Unit: Enum,
       Value: Float
     },
   ],
   Namespace: String
}
```

As you can see, Listing 5-3 shows a basic JSON with a lot of attributes. There are no really complex ones; they're mostly basic types. Table 5-1 shows more detail about the data expected in each one.

Table 5-1. *List of attributes available as part of the metric's data*

Attribute	Description	Required?
MetricData	Contains the data for the metric. This is an array of objects that will hold the information for each metric being reported.	Yes
MetricData/ MetricName	The name of your metric can be anything you'd like. Just make sure it's something that you can understand easily by reading it, so later you can look it up on CloudWatch's console.	Yes
MetricData/ Dimensions	An array of objects, which are simply Name, Value pairs. Your metrics can have between 1 and 10 dimensions each.	Yes, at least one
MetricData/ Timestamp	The time when the piece of metric data was received. It is expressed as the number of milliseconds since Jan 1, 1970 00:00:00 UTC	Not required
MetricData/Value	The actual value of the metric. Note that although the parameter is meant to be a Float, CloudWatch does not support values too big or too small, or special values such as NaN, +Infinity, and so on.	Not required
MetricData/ StatisticValues	An object which contains a set of attributes pertaining to statistics about your metric.	Optional, but if used all of its children are mandatory

(continued)

Table 5-1. (*continued*)

Attribute	Description	Required?
MetricData/ StatisticValues/ SampleCount	The number of sample values used for the statistics reported.	Only if parent element is present
MetricData/ StatisticValues/ Sum	The sum of values for the sample set reported	Only if parent element is present
MetricData/ StatisticValues/ Minimum	The minimum value of the sample set.	Only if parent element is present
MetricData/ StatisticValues/ Maximum	The maximum value of the sample set.	Only if parent element is present
MetricData/Unit	The unit for your metric. It is an enum, so only a set of predefined values can be used here, such as "Seconds" or "Bytes" or "Bits/Seconds". Refer to the documentation for the full list.[4]	No

Based on the data on Table 5-1, we can create a simple metrics module that will help us report data back to CloudWatch. As you can see in Listing 5-4, the code is not complex , and we're not really using all the attributes mentioned in Table 5-1.

---

[4]Please visit https://docs.aws.amazon.com/AWSJavaScriptSDK/latest/AWS/ CloudWatch.html#putMetricData-property for more details.

Listing 5-4. Metrics module using AWS' SDK

```javascript
// Load the AWS SDK for Node.js
var AWS = require('aws-sdk');
// Set the region
AWS.config.update({region: 'us-east-2'});

// Create CloudWatch service object
var cw = new AWS.CloudWatch({apiVersion: '2010-08-01'});

module.exports = {
        report: (ns, metric, dimensions, cb) => {

                var params = {
                  MetricData: [
                    {
                      MetricName: metric.name.toUpperCase(),
                      Dimensions: [ dimensions ],
                      Unit: metric.unit,
                      Value: metric.value
                    },
                  ],
                  Namespace: ns
                };

                cw.putMetricData(params, cb);
        }
}
```

There is very little to get out of that code, since it's pretty straightforward. We're exporting an object with a single method, which basically wraps the putMetricData method from the SDK. What's not being shown in that code, however, is where the credentials to authenticate against AWS are. We're not actually taking care of that directly, because the SDK is doing that for us. All we have to do is to create a file on the server where your app is running, as shown in Listing 5-5.

Listing 5-5. Format of the credentials file

```
[default]
aws_access_key_id = [YOUR AWS ACCESS KEY]
aws_secret_access_key = [YOUR AWS SECRET KEY]
```

That file should be stored in ~/.aws/credentials (or your usual Windows equivalent), and you can get that information from AWS Console, while creating your users or by regenerating these keys (for security reasons the AWS system does not allow you to download existing keys).

After everything is set up and you can successfully test the code from Listing 5-4, Listing 5-6 shows how to modify the original code to start capturing the stat and reporting it back to CloudWatch.

Listing 5-6. Modified code of the main API's code

```
const express = require('express')
const app = express()
const metrics = require("./metrics")

app.get('/', (req, res) => {

        let start = (new Date()).getTime()
        res.send(Date() )
        let total = (new Date()).getTime() - start + (Math.
        round(Math.random() * 100));

        metrics.report('API/TRAFFIC', {name: 'VISITS',
        value: 1.0, unit: 'Count'}, {Name: 'Counter', Value:
        'Requests'}, (err) => {
                if(err) console.error(err);
                else console.log(" - Count stat sent - ")
```

```
        metrics.report('API/TRAFFIC', {name: 'VISITS',
        value: total, unit: 'Milliseconds'}, {Name:
        'PERF', Value: 'DELAY'}, (err) => {
                if(err) console.error(err);
                else console.log(" - Time stat sent - ")
        })
    })
})

app.listen(3000, () => console.log("What's the time API up and
running on port 3000"))
```

Let's break down the code from Listing 5-6, because there is a lot in there, even though it might not seem like it.

I've added all the code inside the request handler; this is for simplicity, but you can refactor it as you see fit. In it you can see I'm just calculating the time difference between the previous line actually getting the current date and the line after it. In other words, I'm just going to be reporting the performance of this endpoint and the number of requests it received (simply by sending the first of the two report calls).

Because this is clearly a very simple endpoint, I'm adding a few random numbers to the time difference calculation, just to add some variability to our results (you'll want to omit that random bit in your own code, obviously).

I'm reporting the data using our wrapper module from Listing 5-4. The parameters seen here are what are important. In both cases, the first one is the namespace. This is key because it allows you to group your metrics in CloudWatch's console. As you'll see in Figure 5-3, both of our metrics will be saved in the same API/TRAFFIC namespace. The second one is the actual metric itself; the first report simply sends a 1, as a count, but the second report call sends the time difference, on milliseconds (see the unit parameter). Finally the third parameter is the dimension; you can have up to 10 dimensions for each namespace and they will allow you to further group your metrics.

Figure 5-3. *Steps navigating through your custom metrics*

Note   You can't use namespaces starting with AWS/; those are reserved for AWS services.

Figure 5-3 shows the steps needed to go through the hierarchy you created by using the namespace and the domains:

1. In the first step, you can see the namespace we defined on our code API/TRAFFIC, and below it, you can see the space for the AWS namespaces (which we're not using right now).

2. The second step will show the domains defined inside our namespace. In this example you can see four, which are tests I made, but two of them are the ones defined in the example of Listing 5-6 (Counter and PERF).

3. Finally, in the third step, you can see the counter we defined for the number of requests. By selecting it, you can add it to the plot on top of this list.

After you're ready with your code and you're properly sending the data up to CloudWatch, you can begin creating your plots Figure 5-4 shows the first one, which is plotting the number of requests received by our API.

Figure 5-4. *Plot of the requests metric*

Simply by clicking on the metric (as shown in Figure 5-4), your data will be plotted into the chart shown. Initially, your plot might not look as you expect; here is what I changed:

- The Statistic column needs to be changed from the default value (which is Average) into Sum; since we're submitting a 1 with every request, that will allow us to get the exact number of requests in the period of time we pick.

- The Period column was also changed; by default it was aggregating data every 5 minutes, and for the purposes of this demo, I wanted a more detailed view, so I changed it to 1 minute.

- Finally, I added a name in the top-left corner of the chart, to make sure that once I add it into a dashboard, I can properly identify the widget.

We do the same for the other metric (see Figure 5-5), but instead of adding up the numbers, we leave the Statistic column at Average, because in this case, we want the average of the delay for all requests received within a minute.

Figure 5-5. *Plot for the average delay*

Caution   Remember that you can do these tests using the free tier of AWS, but if you go overboard with your metrics and alerts, you might start running into costs.[5]

---

[5]See https://aws.amazon.com/cloudwatch/pricing/ for more details about costs of this service.

Adding AWS Metrics into Your Dashboard

Compared to adding your own custom metrics, this should be a walk in the park; but nevertheless it's also something you should be aware of, since it will allow you to monitor your infrastructure.

The great thing about using CloudWatch is that it is very straightforward. Remember the earlier section on the AWS/ namespace? Well, for every one of its services you use, several namespaces will pop-up under this section, letting you pick the metrics you care most about. Maybe you want to look at CPU utilization, or memory consumption, disk read operations, network traffic or a lot of other indicators.

Again, this will happen automatically, so all you have to do is start using your services, and wait a few minutes until those resources finish booting up and connecting (usually no more than 5 minutes). After that, you can go to the CloudWatch console inside the metrics section, and you'll find all the new namespaces waiting for you. Figure 5-6 shows how after starting a single EC2 instance and setting up an RDS MySQL instance, three different official namespaces have appeared.

Figure 5-6. *New AWS-specific metrics appear automatically*

103

As you can see, AWS provides a lot of metrics for each service, so you can make sure you are aware of everything you need for your infrastructure-related metrics. And based on that, you can create whatever scaling rules you need (more on that in a bit).

Reacting to Your Metrics

This is the last step in the process. So far, you've being setting up your monitoring system to look for both custom and default metrics received by your infrastructure and your own Node.js application. You've created at least one dashboard (maybe more), and you can log in into AWS Console any time you want and look at those numbers.

But we want that process to also be automated; it makes no sense to have you, or anyone else, systematically logging in and checking numbers, does it? So instead, let's look at how you can use AWS Console and its services to understand how to automate that process.

Note   For simplicity purposes I'm not going to go into all details regarding this process, especially because AWS tends to update it and make minor changes from time to time. Instead , I'll go over it quickly and let you look at the detailed documentation they provide (and maintain) if you need to know more.

The process can be a bit confusing without an overall guide, but the steps to set up your autoscaling actions based on the metrics you've created so far are as follows:

1. You'll first want to create at least one Alert based on your custom metric (or your default ones, it's up to you). This alert only needs to notify a list of users

when your metrics breach a given threshold. These alerts will be the triggers for the autoscaling actions you'll define next.

2.   You then need to create a Launch Configurator. This component will know what kind of instance to use when scaling.

3.   After that, you'll want to create at least one AutoScaling group, which will have the Launch Configurator associated with it. This group will determine how many instances to create, and will contain the AutoScaling policies.

4.   These policies, in turn, will be associated with the alarms you created in step 1, and they will be configured to either add or remove instances when the alarm is triggered.

That is the basic process you need to go through to automate the reaction to your metrics. Let's now go into a bit more detail on each step.

Step 1: Creating Your Alerts

From within the CloudWatch console, you can create a new Alert, first by specifying the metrics to use, and then by specifying how to treat those numbers (as we did for the charts), as seen in Figure 5-7. You'll have to select the namespace, which will have your own ones and the default ones from AWS. After that, you'll get the list of metrics within that namespace. Simply select the one you want to alert on and the chart below it will update, so you can verify the data.

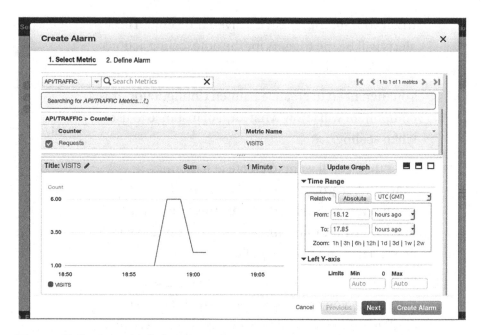

Figure 5-7. *Step 1 of alert creation*

You can play around with the chart in Figure 5-7 as much as you like, even changing the operation to perform on the data (as we did for the Statistic column a while ago) and the time period for the sampling of these numbers. After you're happy with the results, you can move on to the final step, which will take care of setting up the actions for this alert.

Figure 5-8 shows the second step of this process, where you can set the name for the alert and the values to react to (the threshold). Finally, you can select a notification list, or create one on the spot.

Figure 5-8. *Step 2 of alert creation process*

Note   After you're done with the alert, it will appear on your alert list (under the CloudWatch console). Initially this alarm will appear on the INSUFFICIENT list, simply because this alert will take a few minutes to start reporting the data needed. Just wait 5 minutes and the alert should go into another section (either OK or ALARM if it's being triggered).

Steps 2 through 4: Setting Everything Else

Once you have your alerts ready, let's jump on to the AWS EC2 section, since we'll be setting up our autoscaling actions to create new EC2 instances.

On the left menu, under the Auto Scaling section, go to the Auto Scaling Groups section, and create a new group. You'll be prompted to create a group based on a configurator, either an existing one or by creating a new one. If you don't already have a Launch Configurator, then select that option, and you'll be prompted to configure it.

You'll basically be asked to select the AMI to launch when required as well as the type of instance to use for those AMIs. In the end, it will just be a matter of giving this configurator a name, so you can identify it later.

Once you're done with that process, you'll be taken back to the group creation process. Just give the group a name and select at least one Subnet (the rest of the parameters can be left to their default values for the time being).

After that, the next step is to set up your policies. You can leave the group as it is right now and come back to it later, a good option if you don't already have the policies thought out. But if you already know how you want your group to behave, simply add the policies right now.

You'll be prompted for the following items:

1. The minimum and maximum group size, so you'll make sure you don't create too many instances by mistake

2. A name (such as Scale Up and Scale Down for when adding and removing instances)

3. The associated alert that will act as a trigger for this policy

4. The number of new instances to add or existing instances to remove

5. How long to wait between actions (simply to make sure you wait for the new instances to finish booting up before launching new ones)

The next steps are very straightforward; you'll be able to set up notifications when autoscaling takes place, so you can be aware of everything happening at any given time. And that is it; after this step, the rest of the process is optional and not relevant right now. Once your autoscaling group is configured, you're done, and you can start testing it. If you've been following the examples in this chapter, you can boot up your API and send several requests in a row; and if you configured a low enough number on your alert, you'll see how a new instance is triggered for you.

Summary

This chapter addressed the question of when to scale. We also went over a practical example of how to set up one of the main cloud provider platforms to monitor and auto-scale your platform based on whatever metrics you might think of.

In the next chapter, I will cover a topic that even though it is not strictly related to scaling platforms, is very much required for creating applications that are stable enough to scale properly: testing your applications.

CHAPTER 6

Testing Your Application

Let's take a break from discussing architectural patterns and scaling techniques and discuss something equally important for your project: how are you going to test it?

The purpose of this chapter is to give you a little insight into what we normally mean by "testing" in the context of software development. I'll cover some basic principles such as unit testing, mocking, and so forth, and once you're ready, we'll go over some examples of how to implement those concepts in your Node.js project.

So let's get started.

Testing 101

First things first: if by the end of this chapter you want to know more about unit testing, please feel free to go online and keep reading. There is more than enough material about this subject to fill several books. This chapter's only aim is to act as an entry way into this world.

© Fernando Doglio 2018
F. Doglio, *Scaling Your Node.js Apps*, https://doi.org/10.1007/978-1-4842-3991-9_6

The Definition

Let's start with the basics: at its core, testing in the context of software development is basically the act of formulating a statement (something that should be true) about a piece of code and adding the required set of assertions to make sure we can prove that the statement is actually true. So a test can be something like Listing 6-1.

Listing 6-1. Pseudocode for a theoretical test case

```
Statement: "myFunction" is capable of adding up two natural
numbers
Assertions:
var a = 10;
var b = 2;
assertion(myFunction(a, b), "is equal to", a + b)
```

We're not focusing on a specific language right now, so Listing 6-1 shows only a pseudocode attempt at what a test would look like. I should also note that in the example I'm testing the function directly. It is a simple example and there is not a lot of context, but the point is that your tests should focus on the smallest bit of code that makes sense, instead of testing several things at the same time. Let me explain with another example, shown in Listing 6-2.

Listing 6-2. Several assertions in the same test

```
Statement: "myFunction" can add, multiply and substract two
natural numbers
Assertions
var a = 10
var b = 10
assertion(myFunction("add", a, b), "is equal to", 20)
assertion(myFunction("multiply", a, b), "is equal to", 100)
assertion(myFunction("substract", a, b), "is equal to", 0)
```

This example is still quite simple, but I've added a bit more complex internal logic to the function called myFunction by adding the ability to pass in the mathematical function to apply as the first parameter. With this new logic, the function we're testing is bigger, and it does different things, so if we design our tests as in Listing 6-2, we can run into a problem: what happens if our test fails?

I haven't really covered what it means to "run" our tests, but it should be pretty obvious by now: your code is executed and the assertions are verified; if they are true, then your test will succeed, but if they fail (your assertion stated that two values were to be equal and in practice, they aren't), then your entire test fails. You can see the problem if you're testing several things within the same test. Once you get the results back from the execution, you will have to dig deeper into the execution logs (if there are any) to understand where your problem lies.

In order to properly test a function like the new myFunction, you'd be better off splitting your test case (which is how you call a single test) into three different ones (as shown in Listing 6-3).

Listing 6-3. The correct way to structure test cases when the function tested is too complex

```
Statement: "myFunction" can add two natural numbers
var a = 10
var b = 10
assertion(myFunction("add", a, b), "is equal to", a+b)

Statement: "myFunction" can multiply two natural numbers
var a = 10
var b = 10
assertion(myFunction("multiply", a, b), "is equal to", a*b)

Statement: "myFunction" can substract two natural numbers
var a = 10
var b = 10
assertion(myFunction("substract", a, b), "is equal to", a-b)
```

Now whenever a test fails, you'll get better details from your test runner, because you'll know exactly which test failed, and thus, you'll be able to determine immediately which block of code in your complex function failed.

So to summarize and also give you a more *technical* definition of what unit testing is, from everything I've shown you so far, you could probably say that:

> *A unit test is a statement about a unit of code that needs to be proven true in order to pass.*

The word *unit* is the most important one there, because if you go online, you'll probably find a lot of people defining it as your functions (provided you're using a procedural programming language) or your methods (if you're using an OOP language). But as you can see from a simple generic and pseudocode-based example, a *unit* of code can actually be smaller than that. It's true that in all these examples I didn't really show the actual code of the function, and you could argue that for each test case of Listing 6-3, our function is actually calling other, smaller functions, and that is a very good point!

But there is also probably code tying all those calls together (some kind of logic based on the value of your first parameter), so if you were to test those smaller functions individually instead, you'd be missing possible bugs in there. So we can modify our definition of *unit* (in the context of software testing) to something like the following:

> *A unit of code is the smallest block of code that makes sense to test and would allow you to cover a whole logical path.*

So putting both definitions together, you get a pretty accurate idea of what testing your code means and a good basis for the rest of this chapter.

The Tools

Now that we've covered what unit testing is, let's review the tools provided by this methodology that will allow you to test your code.

These are not software tools; they aren't libraries or frameworks you can use. We're not there yet. What I'm trying to give you here are the concepts, the wheels you'll use to build your car down the road.

Test Cases and Test Suites

Test cases have already been covered, but to reiterate, they define how you call the test. You normally structure them to test a very specific scenario, which is why you usually need several cases before you can be sure you've properly covered every logical path in your code.

Test suites are, as their name implies, groups of test cases. Depending on your system and your methodology, you might want to have a single test suite for all your tests or a set of suites, acting as logical groups for your unit tests. The criteria used for the suites are entirely up to you and your team, so feel free to use this tool to organize your code as much as you can.

Assertions

I've already used this concept in the previous section without formally defining it, because it's one of those things you don't really need to define before people can understand it. That being said, there are still some details I left out, so let me cover them here.

Assertions bring meaning to your test cases; everything else within your test is just preparation for these few lines of code. In other words, you first set everything up (function imports, variables, correct values, and so on), and then state your assumptions about the output of the tested code, and that, that is your assertion.

If you want to get a bit more technical, an assertion is (usually) a function or method that executes your target code with the right parameters and checks its output against your expectations. If they match, then the function makes your test pass; if they don't, then it returns an error using the information it has about your test (description, function called, expected value, and actual value are some of the most common ones).

You don't usually need to worry about creating assertions; they are part of every testing framework and library out there. All you need to know is how to use them, and that will depend on each implementation. Usually testing frameworks provide several flavors of assertions to help make the test case code be more readable. So you might find yourself using assertions called `isTrue`, `isEqual`, `notEqual`, `throwsException` and similar names, instead of using just one as in my previous examples. They are, of course, syntactic sugar, but when it comes to test development, making code readable and easy to understand is considered a very good practice.

It is also considered a very good practice with assertions to structure your test cases in such a way that you only have one assertion per test. This will help you do all of the following:

- Keep your test's code clean and simple.

- Make the code readable.

- Simplify debugging when one of the tests fails, because there is only one thing that can fail per test.

Stubs, Mocks, Spies and Dummies

These are all similar tools, so I wanted to cover them as part of the same section since they're all related in one way or another. It's important to note that so far the examples provided in this chapter have been quite simple and naïve. Usually production systems aren't so straightforward, and your methods and functions will normally interact with each other and external services (such as APIs, databases, and even the filesystem), and this set of tools will help you with that interaction.

One key mantra that you need to repeat over and over when writing tests is this:

I shall not test code that's already been tested by others

Even though in theory that's quite obvious, in practice, the line is sometimes a little blurry. One very common case, particularly when writing public APIs, is to use databases. Your CRUD methods, for instance, will most likely be 80% database interaction, so should you test that code? The answer is "not entirely." Look at Listing 6-4 for an example.

Listing 6-4. Generic save function interacting with your database

```
function savePerson(person) {
        if(validationFunction(person)) {
                query = createSavePersonQuery(person)
                return executeQuery(query)
        } else {
                return false
        }
}
```

Listing 6-4 shows a very basic database interaction. It has several functions that you would probably have already tested individually because of their complexity (`validationFunction` and `createSavePersonQuery`), and it also has a function called `executeQuery`, that in our case is provided by your database library. You didn't write that function and don't even have access to its code, so why would you care about testing it? You can't really do anything about it if it fails.

More so, why would you even consider depending on your database server being up and running? Are you going to be using the production database for your tests? What will you do with the garbage data generated by your tests? What if your database server is up, but your table is not created? Will the test fail? Should it?

These are all normal questions that arise when starting to write tests and hitting the brick wall that is reality. If you're not starting out just with tests but with software development in general, you might think the right way to go is to have a "test database," one you can control and you can do whatever you want with. I've done it; it's completely normal, but also **wrong**.

You see, when you add an external service into your tests, even one you think you can control such as your own database server, you're implicitly testing that service and the connectivity between both systems within your unit test. You've turned a simple and straightforward test into a very complex one that is not even prepared to handle everything that could go wrong. What if your network fails? Should this test fail? What if you forgot to start your database server? Should this test fail, too? And this is just one simple example, one database; I'm not covering logging, other APIs, multiple database queries, and so forth. You *definitely* need to cut all connections to the *outside* when unit testing; and that means everything that is not your target unit of code. Fear not, though, because that is where this particular set of tools comes into play.

Tip   When your architecture is complex enough, containing modules that have dependencies with each other, acting as external services, you might want to also consider integration testing, discussed briefly at the end of this chapter, as well as unit testing your source code.

Stubs

Stubs help you deal with external services, by replacing the code that uses them with a simpler version, which instead returns a known and controlled value.

You can stub a function or a method in a particular object (as long as the language lets you), so instead of controlling the database and its content (as in the previous example), you would overwrite the function that does the actual query with one that controls the output as you need it. This way, you can safely test all possible cases, as shown in Listing 6-5 (including those when the network connectivity fails, or the database is down).

Listing 6-5. Pseudocode examples of how stubs help your tests

```
Statement: when the person is saved, the function should return
TRUE
Stub: executeQuery(q) { return TRUE } //we assume the query
execution went well
var person = { name: "Fernando Doglio", age: 34}
assertion(savePerson(person), "equals to", TRUE)

Statement: when the person's data is not valid, the function
should return FALSE
Stub: validationFunction(data) { return FALSE}
var person = { name: "Fernando Doglio", age: 34}
assertion(savePerson(person), "equals to", FALSE)
```

Listing 6-5 shows two examples of why stubs are so useful. The first one shows how you can easily control the outcome of the interaction with an external service. You don't need complex logic in your stubs; the important part of them is their returned value. The second example is not overwriting an external service, but rather, an external function, in fact, one that you would probably have written. And the reason for that (instead of simply providing an invalid person object as input) is that in the future, your validation code could change—maybe you'll add or remove valid parameters to or from your person definition, and then your test could fail, not because of the code you're testing, but an unwanted side effect.

So instead of suffering from that, you simply eliminate the dependency on that function, and make sure that no matter what happens to the internal logic of `validationFunction`, you'll always handle the `FALSE` output correctly.

In fact, both examples from Listing 6-5 show the most common uses for stubs:

1. Removing dependency from external service

2. Removing dependency from communication infrastructure (related to the previous point)

3. Forcing a logical path within your target test code

4. Ensuring that if there is an error, it will be in your code and not an external service.

Mocks

Mocks are very similar to stubs—so much so that many people use both terms to refer to the same behavior. But that is not correct; even though they're conceptually similar, they are also different.

Whereas stubs allowed you to replace or redefine a function or a method (or even an entire object), mocks allow you to set expected behaviors on real objects/functions. So you're not technically replacing the object or function; you're just telling it what to do in some very specific cases. Other than that, the object remains working as usual.

Let's look at the example shown in Listing 6-6 to understand the definition.

Listing 6-6. Example of how a mock can be used in a test case

```
Statement: When replenishing the diapers aisle, the same amount
added, needs to be removed from the inventory
Code:
```

```
var inventory = Mock(Inventory("diapers"))
//set expectations
inventory
        .expect("getItems", 100)
        .returns(TRUE)
        .expect("removeFromInventory", 100)
        .returns(TRUE)

var aisle = Aisle("diapers")
aisle.setRequiredItems(100)
aisle.replenish(inventory) //executes the normal flow
assertion(aisle.isFull(), "equals to", TRUE)
assertion(inventory.verifiedBehavior, "equals to", TRUE)
```

(Yes, that's two assertions in the same test case; I haven't even finished the chapter and I'm already going against my words. Bear with me here; in some cases the expected behavior for mocks is automatically checked by whatever framework you're using, so this example is just to let you know it's happening.)

Now, back to the example in Listing 6-6. We could have definitely done this with stubs, too, but we're *conceptually* testing something different. Not just the final state of the `aisle` object, but also the way the `aisle` object interacts with the `inventory`, which is a bit harder to do with stubs. During the first part of the test, where we set the expectations, we're basically telling the mocked object that its `getItems` method should be called with 100 as a parameter, and that it should return TRUE. We're also telling it that its `removeFromInventory` method should be called with 100 as a parameter and to return TRUE when this happens. In the end, we're just checking to see if that actually happened.

Spies

As cool as this name might sound, we're still dealing with special objects for your test cases. This type of object is an evolution of the stub, but I'm only now discussing it because spies are the answer to the example in the mock discussion.

In other words, spies are stubs that gather execution information, so they can tell you, at the end, what was called, when, and with which parameters. There is not much to them; we can look at another example (Listing 6-7) where you'd need to know information about the execution of a function in order to show you how you could test it with spies.

Listing 6-7. Example of a spy being used to determined if a method was called

```
Statement: FileReader should close the open file after it's
done.
Code:
var filename = "yourfile.txt"
var myspy = new Spy(IOModule, "closeFile") //create a spy for
the method closeFile in the module dedicated to I/O
var reader = new FileReader(filename, IOModule)
reader.read()

assertion(myspy.called, "equals to", TRUE)
```

The example in Listing 6-7 should probably be one of many tests for the FileReader module, but it illustrates when a spy can come in handy.

Note   The spy, unlike the stub, wraps the target method/function, instead of replacing it, so the original code of your target will also be executed.

Dummies

Dummies are simply objects that serve no real purpose other than being there when they're required. They are never really used, but in some cases, such as strongly typed languages, you might need to create dummy objects for your method calls to be possible.

If you're creating a stub of a method that receives three parameters, even though you're not thinking about using them, you might need to create them so they can be eventually passed to the method stub. This is a very simple case of a test utility object, but *dummy* is a term that also gets mentioned quite a bit, so I thought I'd cover it.

Fixtures

Test fixtures help provide the initial state of your system before your tests are executed. They come in handy when your tested code depends on several outside sources of data.

For instance, think of a configuration checker for your system. You could have fixtures for different versions of your config files, and load one in each test case, depending on the type of output to test.

Fixtures are usually loaded before the tests are run, and they can be unloaded (or reverted if necessary) after everything has been tested. Usually test frameworks provide specific instances of the testing flow for these cases, so you just need to have your fixture-related code in place.

Best Practices

I've already covered some of these briefly in the previous section, but it's a good idea to review the full list of recommended practices when writing tests. Like anything in software development, it's never a solo effort; even if you're the only one writing code right now, you have to think about the future.

So let's quickly review and recap:

- **Consistent**: Your test cases need to be consistent, in the sense that no matter how many times you run them, they always need to return the same result if the tested code hasn't changed.

- **Atomic**: The end result of your tests needs to be either a PASS or a FAIL message. That's it; there is no middle ground here.

- **Single responsibility**: This one we already discussed: each of your tests should take care of just one logical path so that their output is easy to understand.

- **Useful assertion messages**: Testing frameworks usually provide a way to enter descriptions of your test suites and test cases, so that they can be used when a test fails.

- **No conditional logic within it**: Again, I mentioned this one earlier: you don't want to add complex logic within the test case; it is only meant to initialize and verify end results. If you see yourself adding this type of code into your test cases, then it's probably time to split it into two (or more) new cases.

- **No exception handling** (unless that is what you're looking for): This rule is related the previous one. If you're writing tests, you shouldn't really care about any exceptions thrown by your code, because there should already be code in place to catch them (unless, of course, you're actually testing that your code throws a specific exception).

Testing with Node.js

Now that you've got an idea of what unit testing is and the basic concepts behind this practice, we can move forward with a specific implementation. You'll see that testing your code in js.Node is not hard at all, even without libraries, since the language already comes with a built-in assertion module ready to be used.

Testing without External Modules

Let me first talk about this option, it's probably not the way to go, since the provided module is pretty basic, but if you're looking for something that's quick and dirty, this will do the job.

One of the major things you'll notice this library is missing is the rest of the framework; with it, you only get the assertion support. The rest will have to come from you or someplace else, but let's look into it anyway.

As I already mentioned, this module does not require any kind of installation steps, since it's already provided with Node's installation. All you have to do to use it is to require the module `assert`. After you do so, you'll gain access to a set of assertion methods, which basically help you compare two values (or objects).

I'm going to list some of the most interesting ones; if you want the see the full list, please go to the official documentation.[1]

ok(value[, message])

---

[1]`https://nodejs.org/api/assert.html`

This method evaluates `value` and if it's true, the test will pass; otherwise it will throw an `AssertionError`. The message (if set) is set as the message of the exception. This one performs a simple equality validation (using ==), so if you need to check strict equality you might want to go with the `strictEqual` method instead.

deepStrictEqual(actual, expected[, message])

This method performs a deep comparison between two objects. That means Node will recursively compare (using the strictly equal operand) properties within the objects, and if that comparison fails it will throw an AssertionError.

For instance, something like what's shown in Listing 6-8 would display an error message.

Listing 6-8. Simple example of how `deepStrictEqual` works

```
try {
        assert.deepStrictEqual({a: 1}, {a: '1'})
} catch(e) {
        console.log(e)
}
```

Listing 6-9 shows the details of the exception thrown by this example.

Listing 6-9. AssertionError exception thrown from the code of Listing 6-8

```
{ AssertionError [ERR_ASSERTION]: { a: 1 } deepStrictEqual { a: '1' }
    at repl:1:14
    at ContextifyScript.Script.runInThisContext (vm.js:44:33)
    at REPLServer.defaultEval (repl.js:239:29)
    at bound (domain.js:301:14)
    at REPLServer.runBound [as eval] (domain.js:314:12)
    at REPLServer.onLine (repl.js:433:10)
```

```
    at emitOne (events.js:120:20)
    at REPLServer.emit (events.js:210:7)
    at REPLServer.Interface._onLine (readline.js:278:10)
    at REPLServer.Interface._line (readline.js:625:8)
  generatedMessage: true,
  name: 'AssertionError [ERR_ASSERTION]',
  code: 'ERR_ASSERTION',
  actual: { a: 1 },
  expected: { a: '1' },
  operator: 'deepStrictEqual' }
```

As expected, because in JavaScript, the number 1 and the string literal '1' aren't strictly the same, the objects compared in Listing 6-8 aren't equal.

Note   If instead you were to use the `deepEqual` method, the comparison from Listing 6-8 would pass correctly.

---

throws(block[, error][, message)

The other method I wanted to highlight is this one, which will test your block of code for a thrown exception. The only mandatory parameter here, is (as the method signature indicates) the first one, but you can also add pretty interesting behaviors using the second one.

For the `error` parameter, you can use one of several options, such as a constructor that simply indicates the type of error expected, or you can also use a RegEx to validate the name of the type, or (and this is as crazy you can get with this method) you can manually check the results by providing a checking function as the second parameter. Listing 6-10 shows a small example taken directly from Node's documentation site, showing how to use a function to check a couple of details about the error thrown.

Listing 6-10. Example using a function as a second parameter

```
assert.throws(
  () => {
    throw new Error('Wrong value');
  },
  function(err) {
    if ((err instanceof Error) && /value/.test(err)) {
      return true;
    }
  },
  'unexpected error'
);
```

There are many other methods to use, but they're simply variations on the three we've just covered, so I'll let you browse the documentation. Let's now look at adding tests in Node using one of the most common libraries, Mocha.

Mocha

When it comes to testing libraries for Node, the list is always growing. You have some that add assertions, others that are full testing frameworks for TDD, others provide the tools you need if you're practicing BDD, and I could keep going. Here I'll focus on the one most people in the community seem to be using these days, and see what testing with it looks like.

Mocha[2] is a testing framework (not just an assertion library, it actually provides a full set of tools for us) that allows both asynchronous and synchronous testing, so considering that asynchronous functions are quite common in Node.js, this is a great choice already.

---

[2]https://mochajs.org/

Installing and First Steps

In order to install the latest version of Mocha into your system, you can simply enter the line shown in Listing 6-11.

Listing 6-11. Installing Mocha

```
$npm install mocha -g
```

This command will install version 5.1.0 as of the writing of this chapter. Once installation is complete, you can proceed to start writing your test cases. Listing 6-12 is a quick example of one.

Listing 6-12. Sample test case written using Mocha

```
const assert = require('assert');
describe('Array', function() {
  describe('#indexOf()', function() {
    it('should return -1 when the value is not present',
function() {
      assert.equal([1,2,3].indexOf(4), -1);
    });
  });
});
```

There are several things to notice from the example in Listing 6-12:

- We're not directly calling Mocha, or requiring the module at all. It is not needed, because to execute the test, you'll be using Mocha's cli tool, which will take care of that.

- We're back to using the assert module from Node, which is one of the features from Mocha: it won't force an assertion syntax on you, it will let you decide which one to use, based on your preferences.

- The describe function can be nested as many times as you need; it's just a grouping mechanism that can help you when reading the code and when looking at the output from Mocha (more on this subject in a minute).

- Finally, the it function contains the actual test case; in its callback you define the test's logic.

To run the test, you simply execute:

```
$mocha
```

And the output should be something like Listing 6-13 (provided you saved your code in a file called test.js).

Listing 6-13. Output from running your Mocha tests

```
Array
  #indexOf()
    • should return -1 when the value is not present
1 passing (7ms)
```

Notice the indentation of the first two lines; that's related to the use of the describe function.

Testing Asynchronous Code

Before going into the specifics of how to test our project, I'm going to talk about one more feature provided by Mocha, since it will come in handy: asynchronous tests.

In order to test asynchronous functions using Mocha, you simply add a parameter to the callback on the function. This will tell Mocha that the test is asynchronous, so it will know to wait until that parameter is called upon (it's going to be a function indicating the end of the test). It is worth noting that this function can only be called once per test, so if you try to call it more than once (or do so by accident), your test will fail.

Listing 6-14 shows an example of what this would look like.

Listing 6-14. Example of an asynchronous test case in Mocha

```
describe('User', function() {
  describe('#save()', function() {
    it('should save without error', function(done) {
      var user = new User('Luna');
      user.save(function(err) {
        if (err) done(err);
        else done();
      });
    });
  });
});
```

The attribute for the callback is usually called done, to signify the ending of the particular test case. Finally, this function follows the normal callback pattern, so it receives the error attribute as the first parameter. Thus the code from Listing 6-14 can be further simplified as shown in Listing 6-15.

Listing 6-15. Simplified example of an asynchronous test case.

```
describe('User', function() {
  describe('#save()', function() {
    it('should save without error', function(done) {
      var user = new User('Luna');
      user.save(done);
    });
  });
});
```

There are many other features for this library that I haven't covered (and won't) in this chapter, so I urge you to go to its main website and browse through its documentation. Let's now look at what it would look like to add some tests to our API project.

Testing: a Practical Example

Let's now apply everything I've discussed so far into a single example. Consider an API project, one that is designed for a bookstore. This is a very straightforward API, so it will have a lot of classic CRUD endpoints. Let's assume this API is using the classic MVC pattern for its internal architecture.

All resources are grouped into controllers, with each one having its own set of actions to perform.

For the purpose of this exercise and to show how you can add tests yourself, I'm going to show how to create tests for the create method of the BookSales controller. This controller simply takes care of listing and creating new resources (new book sales if you will), nothing else, and these actions are simple interactions with the database; so again, there is nothing too complex, since the focus here is on the test cases to add, not the actual code to test.

Let's look at the code in Listing 6-16 first, and then I'll do a quick overview of what's being presented.

Listing 6-16. Unit tests for the BookSales controller's create method.

```
const assert = require("assert");
const restifyErrors = require("restify-errors")
const sinon = require("sinon")
const mongoose = require("mongoose")
const lib = require("../lib");
```

```
describe("Controllers", function () {
    describe("BookSales", function() {
        describe("#create", function() {

            let BookSales;

            //setup all we need for the tests
            beforeEach(function() {
                BookSales = require("../
                controllers/booksales")(lib);
                sinon.spy(BookSales,
                "writeHAL")
            })

            //and tear down whatever we changed
            afterEach(function(){
                BookSales.writeHAL.restore();
            })

            //tests
            it("should return an InvalidArgument
            exception if no body is provided in the
            request", function (done) {
                BookSales.create({}, {},
                function(err) {
                        assert.ok(err
                        instanceof
                        restifyErrors.
                        InvalidArgumentError)
                        done();
                })
            })
```

```
it("should call the save method for the
booksale model", function() {
        //we'll spy on this method to
        understand when and how we call
        it
        sinon.spy(mongoose.Model.
        prototype, "save")

        BookSales.create({body:
        {totalAmount: 1}}, {})
        assert.ok(mongoose.Model.
        prototype.save.calledOnce)

        mongoose.Model.prototype.save.
        restore();
})

it("should call the writeHAL method",
function() {
        //we stub the method, so it can
        actually succeed even without a
        valid connection
        sinon.stub(mongoose.Model.
        prototype, "save").callsFake(
        cb => cb() )
        //we create a simple fake
        "json" property that will be
        called by writeHAL
        BookSales.create({body:
        {totalAmount: 1}}, {json: () =>
        {} })
        assert.ok(BookSales.writeHAL.
        calledOnce)
```

```
                    mongoose.Model.prototype.save.
                    restore();
            })
        })
    })
}       )
```

We begin by creating the groups for our tests. As I mentioned before, these groups can be anything we want; in my case I felt that grouping as Controllers ➤ [Controller name] ➤ [Method name] would come in handy.

After that, for the specific method we're testing here, we'll test the following:

- Make sure it returns the correct type of error message whenever the body for a new book sale is not present.

- Make sure it calls the save method on the model being created.

- Check that after a successful data save on the database, the controller is actually calling the writeHAL method, to create the correctly formatted response.

All three tests have different mechanics. The first one shows you how to use the *done* callback optionally available within each test. If you're dealing with an asynchronous function, that's how you tell it when to stop waiting for a response.

The second test is actually creating a spy on a method, so we can tell whether it was called. Note that in order to create the spy, we're using yet another module, called SinonJS; this particular library works together with Mocha (or any other unit testing framework) and provides the same tools we saw earlier in this chapter: mocks, spies and stubs.

Finally, the third test case is creating a stub, because we need to control exactly how the insertion into the database works. (In this case, we end with a returned value of success as if the database was actually there.) This particular test also does not directly create or restore the spy on the `writeHAL` method for the controller; instead, that happens in the `beforeEach` and `afterEach` function callbacks, which are part of the testing flow executed by Mocha. They're provided to exclude from the test case's code anything that needs to happen for every single test.

Now that we've covered the code, let's quickly look at its output to understand what you should be aiming to see. First, you execute it with the following line, assuming you've added the code from Listing 6-16 in a folder called `tests`:

```
$mocha tests/
```

The output should be something like Figure 6-1.

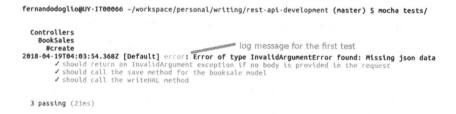

***Figure 6-1.** Output of the execution*

Here you can see the other point of having the groups; namely that the results are much easier to understand if the tests are properly grouped. Also notice the error message; even though the tests are all green, we're showing an error message, and that's completely normal, since the very first test is actually testing for the error type.

Tip   Even if error messages are normal, you still might want to catch them somehow (depending on how you're printing out the error, possibly using a try-catch block, or redirecting the output based on an environment variable) in order to show only messages related to the output of the test, and avoid any clutter related to actual error messages. This could be useful if you have too much clutter from your own code.

Integration Testing

Unit testing helps you save a lot of time and effort fixing bugs later down the road, but when you're dealing with a big enough platform, your modules will start having interdependencies, which in turn means you might run into trouble when they start interacting with each other.

You can have different team members working on different modules of your architecture, and individually the modules can be extremely well tested, but once you deploy them together, you realize that your teams never actually coordinated and have been making assumptions about each other's systems. So once they start sending messages back and forth, your application is no longer working as expected.

This happens more often than you'd think, so having an integration testing strategy from the get-go will save you a lot of headaches in the future.

Testing Approaches

There are different ways to implement integration testing into your system, each with its pros and cons. The most common ones are the big bang, top-down, and bottom-up approaches.

Let's take a closer look at each one to understand when to use them and when to avoid them.

The Big Bang Approach

This approach consists of testing the entire system integration in one go. Forget about module-to-module communication; this approach goes for the entire platform at once.

This is great for small systems, with not a lot of interaction between components, that way if something goes wrong and there is an issue, you can quickly find the root cause for it. If your platform is complex and consists of multi-step interactions between modules, on the other hand, then this approach is not really recommended.

Because you're testing everything at once, finding the root cause of a problem becomes a challenge. you can't simply look at the output of your test and know which module failed; all you'll know is that *something* went wrong, AND then it's dive-into-logfiles time to try to see where the error is.

Figure 6-2 will help you visualize when a big bang approach is actually useful and when it can become a pain in the neck.

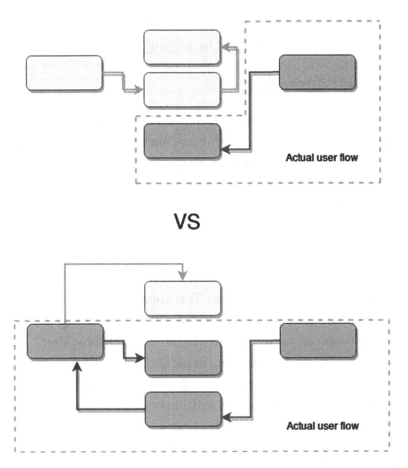

Figure 6-2. *Big bang approach testing entire user flows for simple and complex architectures*

With this approach, finding root causes for issues turned up in the second example of Figure 6-2 would require you to go through the logs of four different modules in the hope of finding out what went wrong.

Another big problem with this approach is that it requires the entire system to be present to start applying it. You can't partially test a user flow if you're going big bang; you have to test the entire thing, so you need to wait for your team (or teams) to have a working version of all required modules before you can start implementing the integration tests between them.

If you're dealing with complex systems, there are other ways to go about integration testing that might better suit your needs.

The Gradual Approach

If testing entire user flows at once is not good enough for your integration testing needs, then you have to go through the interactions gradually, one by one, making sure that just two interconnected systems work correctly with each other, without paying attention to the big picture.

A gradual testing approach can also be broken down (as I already mentioned) into the following:

- Top-down testing, which follows the data flow from module to module, making sure to test the interactions between them in each step. This approach works well if you want to start testing as soon as possible, since all you need are the first two modules of the flow; after that, you can start working in parallel with your devs while they work on the rest of the modules, and you begin adding tests for the existing ones. This approach also works well if you aim to have a quick prototype of your application tested as soon as possible. You don't need all its modules for that, only the critical ones, and this approach allows you to have them tested by the end of the development effort.

- Bottom-up integration testing, on the other hand, starts at the very end of the data flow, testing integration between modules, just like the previous one, but working its way backwards. The main advantage of doing integration testing this way is that problems deep in the integration steps are identified early on. The main problem, though, is that it kills your chances of getting early prototypes out and properly tested if the development flow instead follows a more top-down approach.

In the end, these are all valid approaches, and picking the right one for your particular circumstances requires you to look at your needs, from a development perspective as well as from a quality one.

Summary

This chapter provided a small glimpse into the unit testing world as well as the work required to test big and complex systems. It showed you the basics of unit testing your applications in order to give you a basic idea of what it takes to do that in your own Node.js applications.

In the final chapter, I'll show you some real-world examples of problems experienced by big companies while trying to scale their platforms and how they managed to solve them.

CHAPTER 7

Success Cases

To complete this journey I want to share with you some success cases. As you might have realized by now, you're not the only one having these types of issues; a lot of companies struggle when scaling their successful products, especially when those products are massively successful, like PayPal or Netflix.

In this final chapter, I'm hoping to shed some light into how the big companies are solving the types of problems you and others like you are having.

PayPal

PayPal can definitely be considered one of the early adopters of Node.js for enterprise solutions. Back in 2013 they saw the opportunity to move away from a front-end/back-end type of development group and into a unified full-stack one.

They did this gradually, but started to incorporate Node.js into their team. The first thing they looked at was Express.js, but as happens with many tools, once they started to use it to build their large-scale solutions, they realized it was not enough.

And here is where Kraken.js[1] came in. Their team managed to create a layer on top of Express.js to standardize the output of their different development teams using it. This new open source module is basically

---

[1]See http://krakenjs.com for more details

© Fernando Doglio 2018
F. Doglio, *Scaling Your Node.js Apps*, https://doi.org/10.1007/978-1-4842-3991-9_7

middleware for Express.js, but it adds several features that are very important when creating web applications:

- Lusca provides a layer of security to your microservices. It provides Cross Site Request Forgery, Content Security Policy X-Frame options and more completely out of the box.

- Kappa provides an NPM proxy, capable of creating private NPM repos without having to duplicate the entire registry.

- Makara provides internationalization support on top of Dust.js, which is a templating library. This is perfect if you're not just creating APIs, but also working on the front-end of your application as well.

- Adaro is simply a wrapper on top of Dust.js. It is already in use if you're using Makara, but if you're not, you can simplify your work by using Adaro.

The interesting aspect of this transformation is that because they were hesitant about going all in with Node.js at that moment, once they decided to try it with a new application, they did it by developing the same app in Java as well (which was their language of choice until that moment). They started working on the Node.js version two months after the Java project had started and with just two developers.

The end date was the same, but the Node.js version had around 33% fewer lines of code and almost 40% fewer files. And the cherry on top? The Node.js app was actually considerably faster than their Java counterpart. In fact, you can see the results in Figure 7-1, as published on their technical blog.

Java application

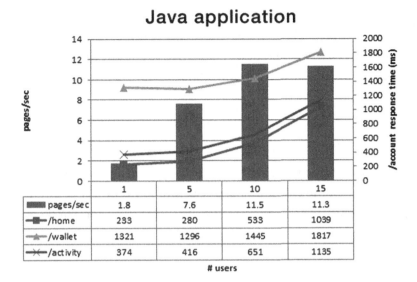

# users	1	5	10	15
pages/sec	1.8	7.6	11.5	11.3
/home	233	280	533	1039
/wallet	1321	1296	1445	1817
/activity	374	416	651	1135

Node.js application

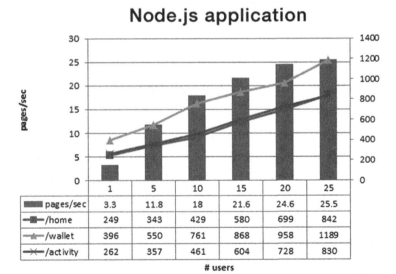

# users	1	5	10	15	20	25
pages/sec	3.3	11.8	18	21.6	24.6	25.5
/home	249	343	429	580	699	842
/wallet	396	550	761	868	958	1189
/activity	262	357	461	604	728	830

Figure 7-1. *Performance comparison between Node.js and Java versions of the same app[2]*

---

[2]Taken from https://www.paypal-engineering.com/2013/11/22/node-js-at-paypal/

In the end, this new approach for PayPal turned out to be a great move. It didn't just increase the performance of their apps (an example of one is shown in Figure 7-1), but it also helped reduce development time compared to their old Java-based workflow.

Uber

This is a company that's been basing their entire business in Node.js since version 0.8. And at the beginning, like any other quick prototype-based production system, they had an architecture like you see in Figure 7-2.

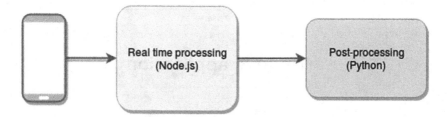

Figure 7-2. *Monolithic initial Uber architecture*

After they started growing out of control and realized this monolithic-based architecture wasn't going to work, they went for a microservices-based approach. The problem? They needed high levels of reliability; the platform had to be up at all times (ideally, it would need to be able to recover from errors on its own) and needed to grow fast and automatically whenever the traffic required it to.

So, because of that particular set of needs, a regular set of microservices wouldn't cut it, in fact, none of the standard solutions at the time did, so they ended-up building their own: Ringpop.

This tool is essentially a library for a Node.js project. By adding it into their code, Uber's developers gained:

- A membership protocol for the nodes of the cluster.
  This works based on a SWIM gossip protocol variation.
  It works very similarly to Redis cluster mode: every
  node of the cluster knows about the others, and can be
  notified if a new one appears, as well as being notified
  when existing members are down. Figure 7-3 shows
  a simplified version of the communication protocol
  and how a new node can notify any existing one to be
  added into the group.

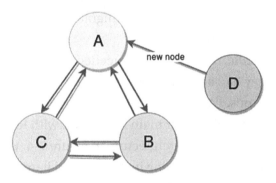

Figure 7-3. *Gossip-based cluster example*

- A consistent hashing mechanism to equally distribute
  workload amongst worker nodes. This makes sure the
  cluster is load-balanced by itself, taking the need for
  load balancing off the developer.

- A transparent "handle or forward" mechanic, which
  makes sure the developer doesn't need to know each
  and every single node of the cluster, instead of that,
  they can simply send a request to any one that's already
  known, and if that node is not able to handle the
  request, it'll forward it to the one that can.

Essentially this library gives the team everything they needed to create an architecture capable of handling the high level of traffic they get every day; and they were kind enough to open source it, so not only can you use it on your own projects, you can also contribute to it and help make it grow and improve.

LinkedIn

LinkedIn is another company that underwent a drastic transformation for some of their services once they started growing massively. But in this case, they didn't migrate off of Java; they migrated from a Ruby on Rails application into a Node.js setup.

To be more specific, the service they needed to grow was their mobile API. At the time they had a single service, which was hit several times per page by the client apps. Each time, a new thread would handle that request (they were using Mongrel as their main web server with RoR). You can see an approximate version of this architecture in Figure 7-4. With their traffic numbers, this was quickly becoming inefficient and hard to scale (each server was quickly running out of memory, limiting the number of threads they could spawn), which is why they took action.

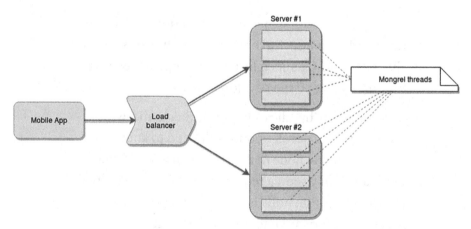

Figure 7-4. *Estimated mobile API architecture based on RoR plus Mongrel*

With Node.js they wanted to move away from that model and into a stateless event-based system, capable of simplifying the interaction between client and server to a single request.

Instead of going for the classic three-tier model adapting the MVC pattern for scale, in this situation they decided to create a different middle tier layer, one that would aggregate all data from different services and send it back to the client. This effectively reduced the number of requests into one, simplifying the logic required on the client app. Even further, they ditched the classic REST approach, and went for a long-lived connection between client and server, able to stream packed data from the server, which in turn, is unpacked and rendered by the client. You can see how this new architecture might have looked like when designed in Figure 7-5.

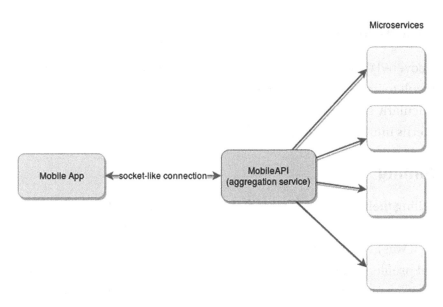

Figure 7-5. *Estimated change on architecture*

With this new setup, they drastically reduced the number of servers they needed, from 30 to only 3, simplifying the effort required to maintain the infrastructure.

> **Note** The comparison here is not meant to state that Node.js is faster than Ruby on Rails, because there are many factors to take into consideration. They didn't just change their programming language and everything started to work; they changed their entire architecture and tech stack.

Biggest Challenges

According to LinkedIn's engineers, some of the biggest challenges they met while changing their entire architecture and tech stack were monitoring and profiling.

Monitoring

We covered this in a previous chapter, and it is not only mandatory, but difficult to implement, since it usually requires ad-hoc setups. This is particularly so when you need to move away from standard architectural patterns into specific models that only suit your requirements.

Profiling

Profiling their applications was also a big challenge and something every team should periodically do if performance is important (which in this case it was). At the time of this change (circa 2012), there weren't many good profilers for Node.js, so they were forced to use what they had at hand and come up with their own workarounds. For example, Listing 7-1 shows a quick snippet of code they came up with to monitor for delays on Node's event loop.

Listing 7-1. Pacemaker implementation monitoring the load of the event loop

```
var oldTime = process.hrtime();
setInterval(function() {
  var newTime = process.hrtime();
  var delay = (newTime[0] - oldTime[0]) * 1e3 + (newTime[1] -
oldTime[1]) / 1e6 - TIME_INTERVAL;
  oldTime = newTime;
  Metrics.PacemakerDelay.update(delay);
}, TIME_INTERVAL);
```

That little bit of code simply adds something to the event loop, recording the time at the moment of insertion, and once the callback is executed, the time difference is calculated. By tracking these numbers, you can keep track of spikes on the event-loop, which would indicate the presence of CPU-intensive code in your application.

Netflix

Finally, Netflix is yet another company that can be considered an early adopter of Node.js. They started playing around with it on an enterprise level early on, and were not afraid of showing their results to the industry once they started putting in production their "experiments."

Like many other companies, by the time they decided to start experimenting with Node.js, they had a full set of monolithic applications written in Java. They were struggling with some aspects of their development flow because of the tech stack in place, having big bulky applications that couldn't really be tested locally, so every time a change was made, it required up to 40 minutes of wait time for build processes and deployment time. And with the constant development of new and more advanced devices, they suddenly were faced with the requirement of supporting all those devices.

Essentially this made it very difficult to expand and grow without a major effort from the development team.

So the first thing they tried was the microservices route; like many others, they went the REST way. Similarly to what the team at LinkedIn ended up doing, they had a REST API in front of a set of microservices. The instant benefit was that they now had a more flexible and standardized interface they could use to add new devices. That was great, but they also had problems, such as having the API and the microservices managed by two different teams, causing the latter to wait several weeks for the first one to approve and adopt their own changes in order to move them into production.

Furthermore, this was one of those cases where REST is not the right fit for the problems. The developers treated everything as a resource (as one should when it comes to REST), but their UI had far oo many resources that needed to be loaded, so every screen required too many round trips before it could load properly.

The next iteration of this approach tried to solve this problem, as well as provide a better dev experience for their maintainers. They needed a more flexible environment, one that would allow them to quickly add device-specific features without the need to redeploy the entire thing. So for this, they came up with API.NEXT, a new version of their API that allowed them to upload new APIs to their server individually without affecting the rest of the teams. You can see a high-level overview of API. NEXT in Figure 7-6.

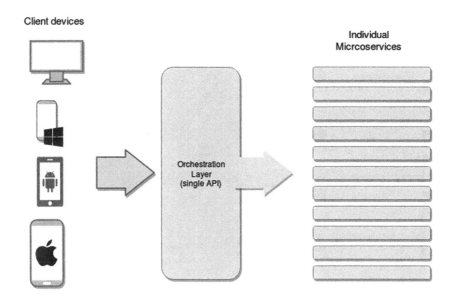

Figure 7-6. *High-level architecture of the approach taken by*
API.NEXT

The problem with this approach was that it quickly got out of hand, and because of the size of these APIs, the team now had thousands of individual scripts to maintain. With all of them being on the same server instance, those servers needed to be upgraded often due to lack of memory, or to handle I/O operations, for example. So all in all, this new approach was definitely a step in the right direction, but they still had several issues to solve.

That's where the final and current version of their API comes into play. For this one, they knew they wanted to keep their developers as a priority but also think about scalability and availability at the same time. So the New Generation Data Access API moved all data accessing APIs into individually running Node.js applications. You can see a high-level overview of this new architecture in Figure 7-7, and you can compare how their architecture changed from the one shown in Figure 7-6.

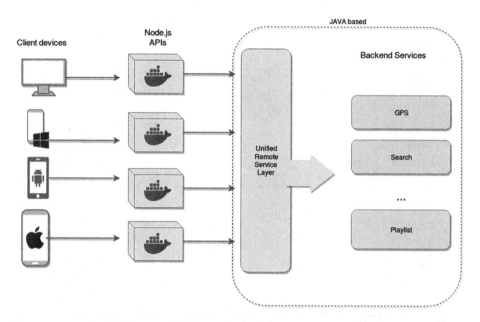

Figure 7-7. *Highly available and scalable new architecture for Netflix's API*

As you can see, they're isolated thanks to the fact they're running inside individual Docker containers. With this approach, they managed to improve their developer's productivity, thanks to having JavaScript everywhere (when it comes to client-facing API development).

Note   This might not be the case for every team, but for this company, it made a lot of sense to have the teams focused on the APIs and the client apps working together as one, and for this, a single programming language made a lot of sense.

Finally, with the Docker approach for their APIs, they also gain productivity since developers can now simply run that container locally and test without having to perform deployments anywhere. One last point to note about this architecture is that it is not purely utilizing Node.js for the entire approach; instead, it's mixing technologies wherever necessary. Node.js on one side makes a lot of sense for APIs, thanks to the speed of development and their easy access to non-blocking I/O. But at the same time, the Netflix team can keep using their Java-based services without having to rewrite them and still get a lot of performance out of them.

Summary

This chapter presented several cases showing how some of the most prominent product-based companies right now have had to deal with their growing pains. Let's recap what each of them did:

- PayPal extended the tools they were using (Node.js) by making sure they can be used at scale because at the time, Node.js hadn't had the attention from the enterprise scene that it has now.

- Uber went from a monolithic architecture into microservices using custom protocols they open sourced.

- LinkedIn went from a Ruby on Rails solution that was not ready to scale (due among other things to the current state of the tech stack they were using) into a custom architecture based on Node.js.

- Finally, Netflix went through a set of changes, iterating over their design, looking for weak points and trying to solve them on the next version. At the end (and possibly something they'll eventually change again) they ended up with a mixed solution, trying to leverage the strengths of each technology without being blinded by just one and using it as a silver bullet.

What you should take away from this chapter, and from this book overall, is this: try to understand how your business is going to impact your product and try to create an architecture that is ready to grow. Take into consideration the industry standards, but don't be afraid to mix and match styles, creating your own solutions specifically tailored to your business needs.

Thanks so much for reading and working through this book; I hope you were able to get something out of it!

Index

A

Adaro, 144
Alerting
    maintenance window, 90
    periodicity, 89
    strategy, 91
    symptoms, 90
    triggering condition, 89
Architecture
    broker pattern, 34–36
    client-server, 25–27
    event-driven, 29–31
    lambda, 37–39
    layers, 20
        data flows, 21
        storage engines, 22
    master-slave, 27–28
    microservices, 32–34
    MVC, 22–25
    patterns, 19
Atomic, 124
AWS Console, 104
AWS ElastiCache, 74

B

Bottom-up integration testing, 140
Broker pattern, 34–36

Byzantine fault-tolerance
    architecture, 16–17
    CRC algorithm, 17
    monitoring modules, 16
    status checkers, 16

C

Client-server architecture, 25
    business-related
        computation, 26
    communication protocol/
        technology, 26
Clustering
    color-coded process, 54
    forking process, 49
    generic API, 50
    install PM2, 56
    IPC, 52
    PM2 logs command, 57
    PM2 start command, 56
    process ID, printing, 54
    single-threaded
        environment, 48
Code Division Multiple Access
    (CDMA), 15
Consistent, 124
Custom alerting strategy, 89

U, V

W, X, Y, Z

Printed in the United States
By Bookmasters